MARY'S
Flowers

MARY'S
flowers

Gardens,
&Legends
Meditations

VINCENZINA KRYMOW

Illustrated by
A. Joseph Barrish, S.M.

with meditations by
M. Jean Frisk

ST. ANTHONY MESSENGER PRESS
Cincinnati, Ohio

NOVALIS

Scripture quotations are from the New Revised Standard Version of the Bible, copyright ©1989, by the Division of Christian Education of the National Council of the Churches of Christ in the USA. Used by permission. All rights reserved.

The excerpt from the "Litany of Mary of Nazareth" is reprinted by permission of Pax Christi USA.

The excerpt from The Rural Life Prayerbook, copyright ©1956, is reprinted with permission of the National Catholic Rural Life Conference.

Cover design and art direction by
    Mary Alfieri
Book design by Sanger and Eby Design

Published in the United States by
St. Anthony Messenger Press
1615 Republic St.
Cincinnati, OH 45210

ISBN 0-86716-349-6

Published in Canada by Novalis
49 Front St. E, 2nd Floor
Toronto, Ontario M5E 1B3 Canada
1-800-387-7164

Canadian Cataloguing-in-Publication Data

Krymow, Vincenzina
    Mary's Flowers: gardens, legends and
    meditations

Includes bibliographical references.
ISBN 2-89507-053-9

    1. Mary, Blessed Virgin, Saint—
Legends. 2. Flowers—Folklore. 3. Flowers
in art. 4. Mary, Blessed Virgin, Saint—
Meditations. I. Title.

QK83.K79 1999   582.13   C99-901265-7

Printed in the U.S.A.

List of Illustrations

Contents

In memory of my parents,
ANTONIA AND FRANCESCO LAFALCE,
whose devotion to "la Madonna" and love of roses,
gardens and all growing things lives on in me.

Acknowledgments

Like the monks of the Middle Ages, I repeat over and over, *Ave Maria, Ave Maria.* Hail and endless thanks to Mary, who has guided me from the beginning of this work. She brought me to all of the persons who have helped me in the writing and producing of this book: Margaret Gallico, who gave me seeds of ideas when she first showed me the Mary's Gardens Nursery catalog; Brother Bill Fackovec, S.M., librarian at the Marian Library, University of Dayton, who first gave me a glimpse of the wealth of Marian materials in the library and continues to find what I need; Sue McCoy, research librarian at the Woodbourne Library in Centerville, Ohio, who negotiated numerous interlibrary loans for me; Father Bert Buby, S.M., who encouraged me early on and whose books have informed my understanding of Mary; my fellow writers in *By-liners*, who inspired and listened and suggested; John S. Stokes, Jr., who encouraged me in writing the book and shared freely his extensive research materials and references; Father Tom Stanley, S.M., Jane McLaughlin, Nan Sears, Eileen Guimond, Miriam Evans and Episcopal Sister of the Transfiguration Mary Veronica, who generously shared information about the Mary Gardens they helped establish, restore or maintain; Sister M. Jean Frisk, whose offer to write meditations for the legends helped form the book; Brother Joe Barrish, S.M., for his willingness to create medieval woodcut-type illustrations of the flowers; Father Johann Roten, S.M., director of the Marian Library, for his help and support and for the translation of Latin verses; my agent, Jim Hornfischer, who saw the potential in this book; my editor, Katie Carroll, who guided the book to fruition; and, finally, my husband Jo, for his encouragement, help and patience.

Foreword

This book is a treasury of Marian flower legends throughout the centuries—retrieved from their diverse sources and collected here that the Blessed Virgin Mary may be better known and honored through her flowers and the legends which so beautifully celebrate her life and mysteries.

In medieval times, each flower had many popular names, changing from locality to locality, many recalling religious legends. However, with the introduction of printing, just one name for each flower, with perhaps an alternate, was adopted for the first "gardening" books; this became the conventional name which has been handed down to us. These arbitrarily selected names were mostly secular and in time came to be accompanied in books by their botanical names derived from the Latin, as plants were scientifically classified. Passed over were some one thousand Marian names for plants, but these continued to live on in oral tradition.

Eventually, these Marian names were linked to the botanical names by botanists engaged in field research. This way, future field researchers would have local names to use when they needed the assistance of residents in finding colonies of plants. It is thus from the "floras" and plant dictionaries of the botanists, and not from popular gardening or religious books, that the principal lists of Marian flowers have been culled.

Folklorists also recorded a number of religious plant names, often with the local legends from which the names were derived. Noting that these religious names correspond to those recorded by botanists, we can assume that many, if not most, of the religious names they used were also at one time accompanied by legends. Still other Marian names were recorded by writers of devotional books.

Of those Marian-named plants for which legends have not yet been found, Johanne Nathusius, in *The World of Flowers: According to their Names, Sense and Meaning* (Leipzig, 1869 translated), writes:

> Legendary stories often provide the explanation for [the
> Marian names]. These legends, and also their outlook, gener-
> ated by a childlike sense for which we no longer find much
> room, are like flower petals blown away from their stems.
> And if the sweet fruit of evangelical truth begins again to
> ripen on these flower stems, then the blown away petals will
> still have as much right as each bloom...to bring us joy.

> Many of the names are explained by legends and associations
> to which, alas, the keys are missing. Is it indeed possible to
> find them again?

We can assume that in medieval times Marian religious flower names and their legends were circulated through the countryside by itinerant preachers, mendicant monks, wandering minstrels, roving players, pilgrims and other travelers, and then handed down in oral tradition through successive generations. This book extends that historical continuity by assembling them from their scattered sources and perpetuating them in modern format.

Other sources have often presented flower legends only as interesting lore; but their vitality and inspiration are, as in medieval times, to be experienced in nature, and especially in the Mary Garden, where the plants are actually cared for and lived with devotionally.

A simple example from my own early experience: When I first read the lovely, childlike legend of the buttercups—that the stars of heaven wishing to glorify the divine Christ Child came down to earth and planted themselves around the Virgin and Child as radiant buttercups—I first regarded it as interesting lore. But the following spring when I next actually beheld buttercups in bloom, the star legend evoked a special devotional joy I had not experienced previously. This experience has been repeated each spring since, with reawakened joy.

As a means of evoking such joy, together with devotional insights, *Mary's Flowers* provides an inspirational description of each legend and its place in tradition, together with an accompanying meditation, with scriptural references. Also illustrating each legend is a medieval woodcut-type color rendition of the flower, as a basis for meditation until you see the blooming flower in the Mary Garden.

For help in planting your own Mary Garden, look at Part Three, "Mary Gardens" on page 146, which includes delightful descriptions of visits to five notable Mary Gardens. There is also an appendix listing Marian names which can help you select the plants that will compose your garden.

John S. Stokes, Jr.
June 25, 1998

Introduction

Mary, wellspring of peace....be our guide.
Model of strength...
Model of gentleness...
Model of trust...
Model of courage...
Model of patience...
Model of risk...
Model of openness...
Model of perseverance....
Woman of mercy...empower us.
Woman of faith...
Woman of contemplation...
Woman of vision...
Woman of wisdom and understanding...
Woman of grace and truth...
Woman, pregnant with hope...
Woman, centered in God....

—FROM THE "LITANY OF MARY OF NAZARETH" (PAX CHRISTI USA)

Mary embodies all the qualities of a holy woman. Whether she is the Mary we knew in our childhood, remembered in the stories told us by the nuns who taught us, the saint in heaven we imagined from holy cards or statues of her, or the Mary we read about in the New Testament, she is a model and source of inspiration for us.

Because she is the mother of God, a mother and a woman, we feel close to her. We find it is easier to have a more personal relationship with her than with the formal, almighty God. So we approach God through Mary. As our understanding of her deepens, she becomes an example to us in our daily lives.

I

As our mother she shows us how to be children of God. Her life journey, like ours, was full of joyful, sorrowful and glorious moments. In those moments she modeled attitudes of happiness, sadness and celebration—all parts of the fabric of life.

The New Testament tells us about Mary's life from the time the angel Gabriel appeared to her. She was a woman of faith. Her willingness to say yes to God serves as an example when God asks what seems impossible of us. Her life was molded by her dedication to the Lord. Even in difficult times, her faith

sustained her. Though there was much she did not understand she accepted God's will. She continued to believe in the midst of doubt. She continued to love and hope in the face of difficulties.

Even though she was pregnant, Mary undertook a long journey to visit her cousin Elizabeth, showing her love and concern for her neighbor and kinswoman.

Mary's Magnificat is a prayer of joy: "My soul magnifies the Lord, and my spirit rejoices in God my savior," and understanding: "His mercy is for those who fear him from generation to generation" (Luke 1:47, 50). It is also a prayer about justice for all people, as she asks God to upset the whole social order and set things right: "He has brought down the powerful from their thrones, and lifted up the lowly; he has filled the hungry with good things and sent the rich away empty" (Luke 1:52-53). Mary is a source of hope for all poor and oppressed people.

Mary was the first disciple and the first Christian. Her experiences as she nurtured Jesus during his early years and walked with him in his final days show us what it means to know pain and suffering as well as joy and tenderness.

When she found Jesus teaching in the temple Mary did not understand what he said to her and Joseph, but brought him home with her and "treasured all these things in her heart" (Luke 2:51). At the wedding in Cana she showed her sensitivity to those in need and her willingness to risk, by asking Jesus to perform a miracle.

Because of her love and continued commitment to her son, she is present at the crucifixion. Full of sorrow and grief, she stands by Jesus until the end. At Jesus' bidding, she accepts his beloved disciple as her son.

Mary is very much with us today. Through her appearances at Fatima, Lourdes, Medjugorje and other places she speaks to us of understanding, mercy, healing and compassion. She shows us the way to God.

We honor Mary in many ways, through the Rosary, special devotions and prayers that help us contemplate Mary's qualities and virtues. In this book we offer yet another way to honor Mary, through reflecting on flowers named after her and immortalized in legends that tell us about her attributes and significant moments in her life and that of her child, Jesus. Through the meditations for each flower we experience these events with Mary and find in them meaning for our own lives.

Thus continues the tradition of using symbols to enhance spiritual life. From its earliest days, Christianity has made use of symbols. Christians recognized each other through signs which helped them conceal their faith and avoid persecution. A lamb or fish represented Christ; grapes and wheat symbolized the Eucharist. Christians also chose symbols to represent God because they could not depict him in human form. A dove represented the Holy Spirit and the peacock symbolized eternal life with its "hundred-eyed" tail suggesting an all-seeing God.

Early Christians, and especially those of the Middle Ages, kept the memories of Mary alive through legends. They saw her attributes in flowers and herbs that grew around them and named them after her. Likening Mary to the "garden enclosed" of the Song of Solomon, they envisioned her in a garden, sometimes called a Paradise Garden, and dedicated gardens to her. These special gardens were filled with the flowers and herbs that reminded them of her.

The tradition of associating Mary with flowers survived over the centuries, kept alive through the Mary names and legends about the flowers, through literature and art.

∽ Development of Mary Gardens ∽ in the United States

Just as in the Middle Ages, when missionaries and wandering minstrels brought stories about Mary's flowers to other lands in Europe, certain people in this country became the bearers of information about Mary's flowers and Mary Gardens. Others who heard about them made it their mission to establish one or more Mary Gardens.

Frances Crane Lillie of Chicago established the earliest known Mary Garden in the United States, on the grounds of St. Joseph Church in Woods Hole on Cape Cod in 1932. During her travels, she had learned about flowers associated with Mary in English monastery gardens and wanted to create a garden in the "tradition of Mary Gardens throughout the world." A chance visit by a priest to Woods Hole in the early 1940's led to a flurry of articles about the Mary Garden there. In one such article in *Perpetual Help* magazine, Father James J. Galvin, C.SS.R., described his joy at finding "Names culled from the merry days when England was Mary's England...when all the flowers of the field were named after her." He continued:

> Scanning the list (posted nearby), you suddenly realized
> that even the flowers you could name, were actually parading
> under false colors. Forget-me-not and campion and fuchsia
> were not their names after all. It came as a revelation that
> foxglove and honeysuckle were our Lady's Fingers. And
> what a world of difference between a name like white
> campion and our Lady's Candles; between forget-me-nots
> and Eyes of Mary!

In Philadelphia in 1951, Ed McTague and John Stokes, Jr., established Mary's Gardens, a nonprofit organization to "revive the medieval practice of cultivating gardens of herbs and flowers which have Marian names." The two men had visited the garden at Woods Hole and thought that the use of flower symbols might be a way of restoring the medieval religious sense to life in our secular age. They researched pre-Elizabethan flower names for Mary and soon had a list of almost five hundred, about one hundred and fifty of them "commonly at hand." They offered seeds, bulbs and plants for Marian flowers through a popular mail-order catalog and published the results of their research in numerous articles. With the advent of the internet, this extensive research was made available to the public on the Mary's Gardens home page (www.mgardens.org).

Today, in addition to the restored garden at Woods Hole, there are public Mary Gardens adjacent to historic Carroll House in Annapolis, Maryland, and at St. Catherine of Siena Church in Portage, Michigan. There are internationally famous Mary Gardens at Marian shrines in Knock, Ireland, and Akita, Japan, at the Artane Oratory of the Resurrection in Dublin, Ireland, and at Lincoln Cathedral in England.

≈ Renewed Devotion to Mary ≈

Devotion to Mary, who had always had a special place in the practices and hearts of the laity, soared after the proclamation of the assumption of the Blessed Virgin Mary in 1950. Pilgrimages, novenas and other prayers, literature and religious art flourished in the years following. Mary Gardens grew in such diverse places as a Montana farm and machine-shop window ledges in Detroit. By one report, there were fewer than two hundred Mary Gardens in the spring of 1951, but several times that number the following year.

Then, in the early 1960's, in the interests of ecumenism, Vatican II cautioned against excesses in devotion to Mary. The understanding of Mary expressed in *Lumen Gentium* was often misinterpreted and devotion to Mary seemed to decrease for a while as theologians struggled to nuance their interpretations. Then, in November, 1973, the United States Conference of Catholic Bishops issued a pastoral letter entitled "Behold Your Mother," presenting Mary as a woman of faith, understood through the study of Scripture. Two important papal documents defined Mary as a "true sister" and a "force for renewing Christian living" (*Marialis Cultis*, "Devotion to the Blessed Virgin Mary," Pope Paul VI, 1974) and a "maternal and active presence" in the life of the Church (*Redemptoris Mater*, "Mother of the Redeemer," John Paul II, 1987), and contributed to the ecumenical dialogue about Mary. Pope John Paul II affirmed that "The Marian dimension of the Church is antecedent to that of the Petrine.... Mary Immaculate precedes all others...."

Biblical, patristic, ecclesial, missionary, liturgical and ecumenical movements stirred interest in the person of Mary and influenced theologians and scholars. Whereas tradition had determined the view of Mary, now Scripture and the Magisterium—the teaching authority of the Church—added important insights.

"The Virgin Mary in Intellectual and Spiritual Formation," a letter from William Cardinal Baum, Prefect of the Congregation for Catholic Education in Rome, stressed the importance of Mary and her mission in salvation history. Quoting from *Redemptoris Mater*, it said, "'Among all believers she is like a "mirror" in which are reflected in the most profound and limpid way "the mighty works of God" (Acts 2:11)' which theology has the task of illustrating."

The 1980's saw a resurgence in devotion to Mary and people who had put aside their devotional practices again sought her at Lourdes, Fatima, Medjugorje and other shrines. Liberation theology, feminist theology, ecumenism and many reported Marian apparitions all served to foster new interest and devotion. Books about Mary have never been more popular, and even mainstream newsmagazines have recently made her a cover story.

❧ About This Book ❧

Mary's Flowers: Gardens, Legends & Meditations is a book about Mary's flowers and the ancient legends that inspired their names. It is a book about devotion to Mary, God's mother and our mother. It shows how we continue to honor her through flowers.

It is a book for reflecting on the qualities of Mary and how they can enrich our lives. The stories about Mary told in the legends can lead to prayer while the attributes of Mary, immortalized in hundreds of flowers, are perfect starting points for meditation.

It is about Mary Gardens, those medieval-type gardens—small, enclosed and full of symbolism—containing flowers and herbs named after Mary, created and cared for in her honor.

Mary's Flowers will help you create a Mary Garden, should you so desire. It can inspire you to select plants for your own garden, which can be as small as a container on your windowsill or as large as your entire backyard.

Part One relates how flowers and plants came to be named after Mary, and how legends about the flowers developed. It describes the place of Mary in the lives of the faithful in medieval times, tells how poets likened her to a "fragrant rose"

and "lily chaste," and shows how the Catholic Church developed a concept of idealized womanhood based on the life and attributes of Mary.

Thirty legends about flowers and herbs which tell of significant moments in Mary's life make up Part Two, the heart of the book. The legends tell of flowers that bloomed when the angel Gabriel came to Mary to tell her she would bear a child, flowers and herbs that bloomed on the night Mary gave birth, plants that performed a special duty when the holy family fled to Egypt, when Mary was raising Jesus and when she stood by the cross at his death. Historical references and botanical data related to the legends and plants are included. A medieval-style color rendition of each flower by Marianist Brother and artist A. Joseph Barrish and a meditation by M. Jean Frisk, member of the Secular Institute of Schoenstatt Sisters of Mary, accompanies each legend.

Part Three includes suggestions for a personal Mary Garden, a herbal garden and an indoor Mary Garden, and prayers for blessing the gardens. Five large Mary Gardens, which can serve as inspiration, are described briefly.

The appendix is a treasury of more than two hundred Marian names of flowers and herbs. It includes botanical names as well as popular names of the plants and information about their naming when available. Flowers and herbs are grouped by how they relate to Mary—her attributes, features, garments; flowers in her household and in her garden; and, finally, a section on Mary's roses.

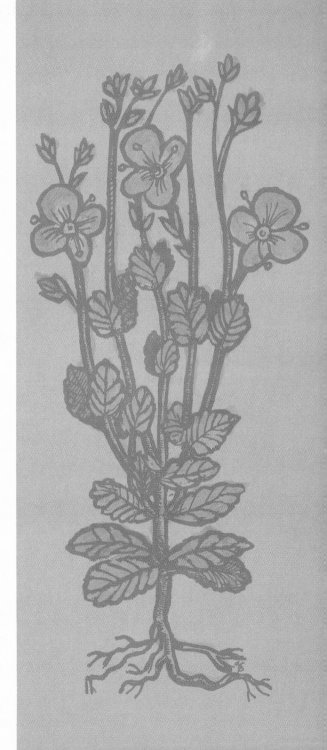

PART ONE

MARY'S GOLD

A History of Flower
Legends and Names

*What flower is that which
bears the Virgin's name,
The richest metal joined
with the same?*

— JOHN GAY

Marygold is the answer to this riddle, one of several by the English poet that show how intimately Mary is associated with flowers. Not only is the marigold named after Mary, but it carries the legend that Mary used its golden blossoms as coins.

It is thought that at one time all flowers and plants honored Mary, the "Flower of Flowers," in legend or in name. The legends were the "offspring of pious thought among pious people." Wishing to honor Mary, people saw reminders of Mary in their daily lives and found special significance in the plants around them. They sought to identify the trees and shrubs named in the Bible and found many connected with events in the life of Jesus and Mary.

The legends survived through oral tradition, since most medieval Christians were illiterate. The legends were not part of the written record of religious and historical tradition, but were later discovered and recorded by botanists and folklorists doing field research.

Mary's flowers have been celebrated in many art forms. Chaucer mentioned the Virgin's Flower (periwinkle) in his poems. Shakespeare wrote that "winking Mary-buds (marigolds) begin to ope their golden eyes" (*Cymbeline*, Act II, Scene iii). Popes and saints called Mary "flower of the field" and wrote hymns associating her with roses and lilies.

In pre-Renaissance art, flowers began to be used in paintings and Mary was painted with flowers of either white or blue—considered her colors. Often she was depicted with lilies, violets or roses. The lily represented chastity, the violet humility and the rose martyrdom, love and heavenly joy. Flowers symbolic of Mary were depicted in scenes of the annunciation, visitation, nativity, visits from the shepherds and the Magi, the flight into Egypt and other episodes in

Mary's life. Roses and lilies appeared in Mary's tomb in paintings of the assumption.

Rose windows paid tribute to her in the cathedrals of Europe. In Florence in the fifteenth century, Luca and Andrea della Robbia's glazed terra-cotta reliefs of the Madonna and Child, many with roses and lilies, were in demand for private devotional use.

Mary was remembered in song. *Es ist ein' Ros' entsprungen* ("Lo, How a Rose E'er Blooming"), based on a fifteenth-century Latin hymn, tells of the Virgin Mother, a rose sprung from Jesse's lineage, who bore the Savior of mankind. An old English carol, "The Cherry Tree Carol," tells about Mary and Joseph walking in a garden and picking cherries the day before Jesus was born.

Numerous legends tell us about flowers and herbs in Mary's life. The angel Gabriel is said to have held a lily (Madonna lily) in his hand when he came to tell Mary that she would give birth to Jesus. The columbine (Our Lady's Shoes) sprang from the earth where Mary's foot stepped when she was on her way to visit Elizabeth. The amazon lily (Star of Bethlehem), carnation (Mary's Love of God), Christmas rose, thyme (Our Lady's Bedstraw) and the oxeye daisy (Mary's Star), are among the flowers associated by legend with the nativity. Clematis (Virgin's Bower), juniper and rosemary all sheltered the holy family during the flight to Egypt, protecting and hiding them from Herod's men. And there are more.

Early Christians found stories about the life of Mary and her son in the Protoevangelium of James in the New Testament apocrypha. It tells about the early life of Mary, her birth, her early years in the temple, the priests' decision (when Mary was twelve) that she should marry, and how Joseph was chosen when a dove came from his staff and rested on his head. James tells about the angel appearing to Mary, Joseph's reaction on finding that Mary was pregnant, and Joseph and Mary's journey to Bethlehem. He tells about the midwife who watched while a great light shone in the cave and Jesus appeared and took to his mother's breast. Certain flowers were associated with many of these events. The Madonna lily and violet were present at the annunciation, the manger herbs shone with a golden light when Jesus was born and the Christmas Rose bloomed that night.

In the thirteenth century, Jacobus de Voragine, a Dominican priest in northern Italy, compiled the folklore of Mary and the saints in his *Golden Legend*. In medieval usage, the word *legend* meant lesson or reading, and Voragine's book was a layman's lectionary of the lessons about Mary and the saints which were read on their feast days.

Other legends developed when monks and nuns in European monasteries and convents wrote stories and plays to entertain and inspire each other. Mystery plays celebrated events in the life of Jesus, Mary and the saints, and the nativity crèche was recreated at Christmas time, inspiring the retelling of old legends and creation of new ones.

Saint Francis of Assisi (1182-1226), known for his love of nature as well as animals, is thought to be responsible for many of the legends. These stories flourished in the thirteenth and fourteenth centuries in Europe and England, falling into disuse as the Reformation and Renaissance took hold in the sixteenth century. But interest in plant symbolism continued during the Renaissance and in succeeding centuries, so some of the legends remained. In some cases the name remains though the legend has been lost.

Each country developed its own legends. German legend says that the carnation bloomed on the night of Jesus' birth. French tradition tells of the sainfoin (holy hay) blooming and circling Jesus' head as he lay on a bed of the hay. A ballad from Somersetshire in England tells of the Holy Thorn:

> The staff het budded and het grew,
> And at Christmas bloom'd the wholdaroo (wonder),
> And still het blooms at Christmas bright
> But best tha zey at dark midnight.

England became known as "Mary's Dowry" during the Middle Ages because of its devotion to Mary and its many shrines to her. Thomas Arundel, Archbishop of Canterbury, wrote in 1399 that "...we English, being the servants of her special inheritance and her own Dowry, as we are commonly called, ought to surpass others in the fervour of our praises and devotion." Devotion to Mary was kept alive through the flower legends.

Legends were carried from one part of the Christian world to other places by missionaries, Crusaders and wandering minstrels, sometimes changing in the retelling. The eastern European tradition of the rustling of the leaves, when the thorn trees blossom on Christmas night to commemorate the Christ Child's birth, was carried to Hampshire, England, where the country folk added their own symbolism. And when they heard the leaves rustle at midnight the people would rush to the nearest cow stall to watch the animals rise and lie down on their other side, reenacting the legend that on the night of the Nativity the oxen knelt.

⧉ Plants Named After Mary ⧉

In addition to those flowers and herbs honoring Mary through legend are the many flowers named after her. Early Christians believed that fragrant herbs and flowers reflected Mary's spiritual sweetness, soothing and healing herbs reflected her heavenly mercy, while bitter and sour herbs mirrored her bitter sorrows.

The Scotch rose and other roses were associated with Mary, the Mystical Rose of Heaven. Lemon balm was called Sweet Mary and thyme was the

Virgin's Humility. Rue was the Herb of Grace, based on the use of its branches for sprinkling holy water, but was also associated with bitter regret, sorrow and pain of loss because of its acrid, pungent fragrance and taste. Meadow rue with its little blue flowers was called Our Lady's Rue, possibly because of the association of the color with sorrow and mourning. The deep purple blue blossoms and the sword-pointed leaves of blue flag iris gave the plant the name Mary's Sword of Sorrow. Dandelion and sorrel were known as Mary's Bitter Sorrow.

During the first century, heathen temples were transformed into Christian churches, and traditions once associated with heathen deities were transferred to Mary and the saints. Plants once dedicated to Venus, Roman goddess of Spring, were rededicated to Mary. The rose and lily, sacred symbols of Venus, became Mary's flowers. *Capillus Veneris* (Venus's hair) became maidenhair fern or Our Lady's Hair.

When Christianity reached Germany and the Scandinavian countries, flowers dedicated to Freyja, the "gladsome, gladdening, sweet, gracious" goddess of love and beauty, were appropriated for Mary. *Frauen-schuhli* (sweet clover) became Our Lady's Shoes; *Fraua-menteli* (lady's mantle) became Mary's Mantle or Our Lady's Mantle.

In medieval times, when spiritual life and daily life were intertwined, it was common practice to give Mary names to everyday items, such as Our Lady's

Flannel (bugloss), Our Lady's Cushion (sweet william) and Our Lady's Smock (cuckoo flower). Some flowers were named because they reminded of Mary's features: Our Lady's Fingers (honeysuckle and lamb's ear); her garments: Our Lady's Mantle (morning glory); or household articles she may have used: Our Lady's Pincushion (sea pink or thrift). Others reflected on her qualities: Our Lady's Modesty (sweet violet), or aspects of her life: Our Lady's Tears (lily of the valley).

In France the ancient Abbey of Cluny, built in the twelfth century, bears a figure of the Blessed Virgin, around which is found this hexameter: "Springtime's first flowers first give thee honors."

Late in the twelfth century Durandus, bishop of Mende, France, declared that flowers were emblems of goodness and recommended that people deck themselves with blossoms, olive branches and palms on Palm Sunday to signify the virtues of Christ. The olive represented Christ's role as peacemaker and the palm was a sign of victory. This is one of the many ways symbolism was used to help the faithful, especially those who could not read, to understand the teachings of the Church.

Plants were dedicated to Mary because they may have been connected with some event in her life or flowered around the time of one of her feast days (snowdrops for the Feast of the Purification and assumption lily for the Feast of the Assumption) and were used in decorating the altar on these days. The Italian aster, which blooms at the time of Mary's traditional birthday, September 8, is known as Our Lady's Birthday Flower.

These lines from an old verse show how flowers were connected with Mary, the saints and events in the Christian year:

> The Snowdrop, in purest white arraie,
> First rears her head on Candlemas daie;
> While the Crocus hastens to the shrine
> Of Primrose love on St. Valentine.
> Then comes the Daffodil, beside
> Our Lady's Smock at Our Lady-tide.
>
> From Visitation to S. Swithin's showers,
> The Lillie White reigns Queen of the Floures;
> And Poppies, a sanguine mantle spred
> For the blood of the Dragons Margaret shed.
> Then under the wanton Rose, agen
> That blushes for Penitent Magdalen.
>
> When Mary left us here below,
> The Virgin's Bower is in full blow.

Monks and poets compared Mary to lilies, roses, violets and many other flowers. In the sixth century Saint Bede wrote that the translucent whiteness of the petals of the white lily symbolized the purity of Mary's body and the gold of its anthers the glory of her soul as she was assumed into Heaven. Writing in the early fourteenth century, Dante called Mary "the Rose, in which the divine Word became flesh...." An early fifteenth-century *Ave Maria* proclaimed: "Heil be thou, Marie, that art flour of all / As roose in eerbir so reed."

⁀ Mary in Medieval Life ⁀

The Church and the world were one in medieval times—"a single, God-oriented organism in which churchmen and lay lords each had appropriate roles to play."

Mary was so much a part of the life of the people that she was daily and routinely honored in legend and with flowers. Christians gathered flowers and herbs for their church, placing them on the altar and strewing them throughout the church on special occasions. Garlands and crowns of flowers were worn by the priests.

Some of the flowers grew wild, others in small gardens near the kitchens of the people. Later the flowers and herbs were grown in sacristans' gardens near the church to provide a constant source of flowers for the altar and for processions.

Poets, especially German poets, "ranged widely through the fields in their search for blossoms which by their beauty or by their healing virtues were fit to symbolize the Virgin," according to one historian.

Roses and lilies were the great devotional flowers of the Middle Ages. They are celebrated, together with violets, in a medieval carol to the Blessed Virgin:

> O fragrant rose, lily chaste,
> O violet of purity,
> Thine eye of grace upon us cast,
> *Noster misericorde.*

During the high middle ages (1050-1300), the Church developed a concept of idealized womanhood based on Mary, symbol of purity and maternal compassion. Mary became the subject of miracle stories and many of Europe's great cathedrals were dedicated to *Notre Dame*—Our Lady.

The cloistered (enclosed) garden came to represent the purity of the Virgin Mary. In the twelfth century this verse—"A garden locked is my sister, my bride, / a garden locked, a fountain sealed" (Song of Solomon 4:12)—became a symbol of the Blessed Virgin Mary.

A description of a garden at Wherwell Benedictine nunnery in England, where Euphemia was abbess from 1226 to 1257, includes this reference to Mary in a garden: "She built a place set apart for the refreshment of the soul, namely a chapel of the Blessed Virgin, which she adorned on the north side with pleasant vines and trees."

The works of writers and artists of this time point to a connection between Mary and gardens. The beauty of roses, lilies and flag iris was extolled by Walafrid Strabo, abbot of Reichenau on Lake Constance (in central Europe), who in 840 wrote poetry inspired by his garden: "*Hortulus,*" or "The Little Garden," consists of twenty-seven poems, each devoted to one plant. Eighteen of the plants also appear in Charlemagne's "*Capitulare.*"

In his treatise on vegetables and plants, written about 1260, Albert Magnus, a count and a Dominican, wrote that "pleasure gardens" should be planted with sweet-smelling herbs and "all sorts of flowers, as the violet, columbine, lily, rose, iris and the like." All of those flowers are associated with Mary.

Artists first began to depict Mary with flowers in the twelfth century and by the fifteenth century numerous paintings showed Mary in flower gardens, many of them enclosed gardens. Some drawings or woodcuts |of Mary in a small garden were titled "Mary Garden," from which comes the name Mary Garden for gardens filled with Mary's flowers.

A small twelfth-century painting in the university library in Ghent, Belgium, shows Mary with leaves and blossoms. In "Virgin in the Rosery" by Stefano de Verona (1375-1438), housed in a museum in Verona, Italy, Mary is surrounded by a trellis of white and red roses.

An early fifteenth-century painting by an Upper Rhenish master, "The Virgin and the Strawberries," shows Mary seated on a bench of strawberry plants. Lily of the valley, violets and snowdrops are in the foreground while red and white roses climb trellises behind her. All of the flowers are symbolic of Mary. The painting is in the Kunstmuseum in Solothurn, Switzerland.

In the mid-fifteenth century Stefan Lochner depicted Mary with roses and carnations in a number of paintings: "The Madonna in the Rose Bower" and "The Virgin Mary with the Infant Jesus," in the Wallraf-Reichartz Museum,

Cologne, Germany; "Mary in the Rose Arbor," in the Alte Pinakothek, Munich; and with violets in "Mary with Violets," in the Munich museum.

"The Virgin of the Rose Garden" by a Flemish Master of the Saint Lucy Legend, painted between 1480-85, depicts Mary in an enclosed rose garden lush with strawberries, carnations and other flowers symbolic of Mary.

Lilies appear in paintings of the annunciation (such as "Annunciation," by Martin Schongauer [1450-91], on the main altar of the Dominican church in Colmar, Germany) and Mary is often depicted in enclosed gardens. "The Annunciation" by a follower of Rogier van der Weyden (c. 1460), in the Metropolitan Museum of Art, New York, shows Mary in a castle garden and "Virgin of the Rose Trellis" (c. 1470), by the Maitre Alsacien, in the Museum, Strasbourg, France, shows Mary in an enclosed garden, holding a rose, with a rose trellis above a low brick wall behind her.

Jan van Eyck painted the Madonna with flag iris and Madonna lilies in a terrace garden ("Madonna with Chancellor Rolin" [c. 1425], Louvre, Paris). Roses, flag iris and lilies of the valley are seen in his "The Madonna of the Fountain" (1439), Musee Royal des Beaux-Arts, Antwerp, Belgium.

∞ Mary, Roses and the Rosary ∞

Roses have long been associated with Mary. One of the earliest legends, from the second century, tells that when Mary was assumed into heaven, lilies and roses were found in her tomb. The pagan rose, celebrated in Hellenic poetry and sacred to Venus, became the flower of the Virgin Mary, who was known as the Rosa Mystica, and a symbol of mystical devotion in the fourth century.

To Christian mystics the white rose typified the Virginity of Mary. As the early Church fathers promulgated the doctrine of the Virgin Birth, they began to associate Mary with "the most perfect of flowers"—the rose. The perfect rose became a symbol of the Queen of Heaven. The cult of the Virgin began in the sixth century and by the seventh century the cult of Mary the Virgin and the Mystical Rose flourished.

Early Christian poets saw Mary's motherhood as enclosing heaven and earth within her womb, symbolized within the space of a single round rose. They associated Mary with the rose and the sealed garden of roses and lilies described in the Song of Solomon: "I am a rose of Sharon, / a lily of the valleys" (Song of Solomon, 2:1).

Rose legends proliferated, reaching a peak in popularity in the twelfth century. A legend that a rose sprang up every place she and Joseph rested on the flight into Egypt connects Mary with the Rose of Jericho, also known as Mary's Rose.

A story about the assumption of the Virgin Mary describes the miracle when Mary's body was laid in the tomb: "And anon she was environed with flowers of roses." The legend of the rose garden in Subiaco, Italy, said to have been planted by Saint Benedict (c. 480-544), tells of Saint Francis of Assisi visiting in 1216 and transforming into roses the bed of thorns which Benedict had used to mortify his flesh.

Several paintings by the Italian painter Botticelli (1444-1510) depict Mary with roses. In "Coronation of the Virgin," in the Uffizi Gallery in Florence, a cloud is edged with roses. Roses appear in "Madonna and Child," at the Louvre, and "Madonna and the Two St. Johns" in the Kaiser Friedrich Museum in Berlin.

Three colors of roses were deemed especially appropriate in a Mary Garden: red roses to symbolize the sorrows of Our Lady, white to symbolize her joys and yellow to symbolize and herald her glories.

The word "rosary" originally meant a rose garden and later referred to a garland of roses. The devotion known as the Rosary, a garland of prayers in honor of Mary, began in the twelfth century.

The Rosary as we know it today has its origin in the "fifties," or Little Psalter, a collection of three sets of fifty psalms used by Irish monks for their devotions. The monks used beads to help them keep count. In the early days of Christianity, monks in the desert used pebbles or seeds to help them keep count, placing them in a basket and removing them as they said each prayer.

In the eleventh century, the Psalms were replaced by Hail Marys, which first appeared in 1050. By the twelfth century the Hail Marys recited on beads were called a rosary and later the beads themselves were called a rosary. Legend has it that in the thirteenth century, as early as 1208, Saint Dominic's prayer beads were called the rosary and that he and his followers spread the devotion in Europe, but religious scholars dispute this. Two different practices of the rosary in the fifteenth century come closer to the rosary as we know it today. The rosary of Dominic the Carthusian in Germany was a succession of one hundred and fifty Hail Marys, each representing a moment in the life of Jesus and Mary. Alain of Roche in France is thought to be the author of three groups of mysteries (joyful, sorrowful, glorious); this list of fifteen mysteries became the norm between 1480 and 1500 and continues as the rosary we know today.

The connection between the rose garden and the rosary beads was made in the twelfth and thirteenth centuries in Europe, and rose gardens became places of meditation and honor to Mary.

Monks had continued to plant herbs and flowers for medicinal use and to decorate altars. Trying to replicate paradise, they created Paradise Gardens.

These enclosed, circular gardens were also known as rosaries, or rose gardens, and became the perfect site for devotion to Mary.

During this time collections of songs, prayers and hymns began to be called flower gardens. People said prayers of a *hortus deliciarum* (garden of delights), a *hortulus animae* (little garden of the soul) and a *rosarium* (rose garden). A collection of hymns of praise to Mary became known as a *rosarium*, or rosary.

PART TWO

MARY'S FLOWERS & THEIR LEGENDS

Madonna Lily

Lilium candidum
Annunciation Lily

Also known as Virgin Lily and Mary Lily

(P)

∞ Meditation ∞

Why shall a lily represent this hour? The lily's upright cup is open as a vessel, ready to receive, strong, fragrant, turning gently to the light. The Galilean lily endured the desert steppe. Once upon a time, the lily from the Song of Solomon was used as a symbol of Mary's undivided availability for God; she is ever-virgin mother overshadowed by the Holy Spirit, open and ready for his overflowing grace.

Mary, seven times you speak in Scripture. Seven "words" for me to ponder. I hear you ask the angel a well thought-out question. You do not ask why; you ask instead, "How can this be?" Your response affirms your trust: With God nothing is impossible. Mary, it is your openness to Eternal Love that makes you remembered—and your response. Do I have your openness to the divine? Do I have your lily-like strength?

∞ Legend ∞

The archangel Gabriel held a lily in his hand in recognition of Mary's purity when he appeared to the young virgin to tell her that she had "found favor with God" and would conceive and bear a son and give him the name Jesus. After Mary touched the flower, which had been scentless, an exquisite fragrance arose from it.

Mary, who was fourteen years of age and betrothed to Joseph, had gone out at dusk that evening in March to draw water from the well near her home. She heard a rustling and then a voice saying, "Greetings, favored one. The Lord is with you." Troubled at the words, she looked around and, seeing no one, went back to her house and continued weaving a robe of purple linen. It was then that Gabriel appeared to tell her about God's plan for her.

The lily symbolizes "white purity and grace, like Mary, pure and full of grace." The writings of the Venerable Bede (673-735), Benedictine monk, historian and scholar, include this poetic description of the Madonna lily as the emblem of the Virgin Mary:

> the white petals signifying her bodily purity,
> the golden anthers the glowing light of her soul.

Chaucer called the lily the "Floure of Virgins all," a reference to the Virgin Mary.

The lily was associated with the annunciation in Italian art early in the fourteenth century, especially in Florence, which had the lily as its emblem. During the fourteenth and fifteenth centuries, the lily was sometimes depicted being carried by the archangel Gabriel. Later a vase of lilies, signifying Mary's purity, stood at her side. A lily in a pot in a scene depicting the annunciation signified that Mary's virginity remained intact even though she was to become the Mother of God.

In the "Annunciation" attributed to Pietro di Giovanni Ambrosi, the angel holds three lily stalks to symbolize Mary's purity before, during and after the conception of her son. The fifteenth-century "Annunciation" by Martin Schongauer, on the main altar of the Dominican church in Colmar, Germany, depicts Mary standing before a vase of white lilies while the archangel Gabriel holds a staff.

The Madonna lily is thought to be the "lily among brambles" of the Song of Solomon. Saint Bernard of Clairvaux, French abbot and spiritual writer of the twelfth century, identified the lily with the Virgin Mary and believed that she was the speaker of the words, "I am a rose of Sharon, a lily of the valleys," from that same book.

It is said that the lily sprang from the tears of Eve when she was expelled from the Garden of Eden and that it had been yellow until the day that the Virgin Mary stooped to pick it.

In 1043 in Navarre, Spain, it was discovered that the image of the Virgin Mary holding the infant Jesus in her arms had miraculously issued from a lily. Garcias, the sixth King of Navarre, instituted the Order of "Our Lady of the Lily" in honor of the wondrous occurrence.

The lily grew in Egypt and Crete in the centuries before Christ and was also found in Turkey and Greece. The Romans introduced it to southern Europe, and the Crusaders are also said to have brought the flower back with them. Known as the lily of Israel, the plant can still be found growing wild in remote places in northern Israel and Lebanon. In England lilies were used for "garnishing" or decorating the churches on all the feasts of our Lady.

The plant blooms in late spring and early summer, often around May 31, the Feast of the Visitation, which commemorates Mary's visit to Elizabeth following the archangel Gabriel's appearance to her.

Another symbol of the annunciation is the maiden's blush rose or incarnation rose (*Rosa alba rubicunda*), which in legend turned from white to pink when Mary blushed at the archangel's words. The amazon lily (*Eucharis grandiflora*) is also called the Madonna lily.

Madonna Lilies are found in the Garden of Our Lady at St. Joseph's Church in Woods Hole on Cape Cod (the first Mary Garden in the United States), and the Mary Garden adjoining the historic John Carroll House and St. Mary's Church in Annapolis, Maryland.

"As a lily among brambles,
so is my love among maidens."

— SONG OF SONGS 2:2

Violet

Viola odorata
Our Lady's Modesty
(P)

∽ Meditation ∽

Wild violets have taken over a corner of my garden. Amazing. Year after year, they conquer a bit more space. In spring they form a profuse carpet of royal purple and lush green. I remember when there was only one fragile plant, humble and hidden. I was certain it would not survive the summer's hot winds. Now there are hundreds of them, a miracle of beauty.

The wild violets remind me of the value of one deed done in humble, quiet acquiescence, a hidden thing, unnoticed to the world. Mary, your yes was such a deed—"Let it be with me according to your word"—one deed, one seed, a total commitment, hidden, calm, fruitful, the finest apparel ever to clothe humankind. Now there is no end to the splendor of your fruitfulness, Jesus Christ among us. If only you could be thanked as you ought to be!

⤳ Legend ⤲

The violet blossomed outside the Virgin Mary's window when she spoke the words, "Here am I, the servant of the Lord," to the angel Gabriel and accepted God's plan for her. Gabriel had come to tell her she would bear the son of God. Humbly and courageously Mary accepted, saying "Let it be with me according to your word."

It is told that as the angel left Mary, he stopped to bless the little flowers, bestowing a delicate fragrance on them.

Long before the angel's visit to Mary, ancient Greeks and Romans considered the violet a symbol of modesty and simplicity. Later many religious writers called Mary the violet of humility. The flower is said to be named "Our Lady's Modesty" because of the modest manner in which the rich purple blooms nestle among the leaves.

Twelfth-century monks and poets saw Mary's virtue in the violet. Saint Bernard of Clairvaux speaks of Mary as the violet of humility in his *Vitis Mystica*. He called the flower the "emblem of humility" because it is small, grows low to the ground, has a sweet fragrance and a dull color. Hugh of St. Victor wrote of Mary, "You are the flower for your beauty....the violet for your humility."

In *Goldene Schmiede, a poem of praise to the most holy Virgin*, Konrad von Wurzburg (d. 1287) compared Mary to the hidden violet.

The violet was considered the third flower in the trinity of medieval symbolic flowers, following the rose and lily. It became associated also with purity, as in this quatrain from a medieval carol to the Blessed Virgin:

> O fragrant rose, lily chaste
> O violet of purity
> Thine eyes of grace upon us cast,
> *Noster misericorde*   [Our merciful one]

Violets were used to decorate altars where Mary's statue stood. The violet was said to have dropped its head when the shadow of the cross fell on it the day of the crucifixion.

In the painting "Madonna of Humility" by Giovanni di Paolo, violets are depicted around the Virgin Mary. Elizabeth greets Mary in the midst of violets, roses and other flowers in a painting of "The Visitation" by a Master of the Retablo of the Reyes Catolicos in fifteenth-century Spain.

Violets were grown in medieval gardens along with roses, lilies, jasmine, hyacinths and lilac. They were found in Paradise Gardens, where Mary was depicted in an enclosed garden, a *hortus conclusus*, symbolizing her Virgin birth. They can be seen in the Bonnefont Cloister herb garden, representative of medieval monastic kitchen and infirmary gardens, at The Cloisters, a division of the Metropolitan Museum of Art in New York City.

Purple violets are known as March violets because they bloom early in the spring. They are found in the Garden of Our Lady at St. Joseph's Church in Woods Hole. There a statue of "The Virgin" sculpted by Vinol M.S. Hannell, depicts Mary as she might have appeared at the moment of the annunciation, head slightly bowed, her expression one of peace and serenity. The concrete statue is more than sixty years old.

Violets also grow in the Mary Garden at the Shrine of Our Lady of Lourdes Grotto in Dayton, Ohio; and the Mary Garden at the Episcopal Convent of the Transfiguration in Cincinnati, Ohio. In the latter, primarily a shade garden, we also find the white violet (*Viola canadense*), called Mary's Delight. Violets are also found in the Garden of Our Lady at the Knock Shrine in County Mayo, Ireland.

"...(They) should dress themselves modestly and decently in suitable clothing...with good works, as is proper for (those) who profess reverence for God."

— 1 TIMOTHY 2:9-10

Columbine

Aquilegia vulgaris
Our Lady's Shoes

(P)

✄ Meditation ✄

Some gardeners slip their shoes off when they work in the garden. The warm earth has its own velvet feel. We become part of it. Some fear the thorn and crawling things, but even through their slippers and shoes, they feel the gentle response of the earth.

Mary, legend has it that you lived your end days with John—some say in Jerusalem, some say Ephesus. How many miles you walked upon this earth! No matter, your grace-filled being brought the Son of Man close to us. Had we lived then, we could have held him in our arms as you did, and cherished him with our hearts. Have we ever thanked you for the role you played? Let us follow your footsteps; even better, teach us to walk in your shoes. Peter denied him; you bore him to the cross; and you bear him even now. For the rest of our days, let us walk with him in the garden.

❧ Legend ❧

The tiny flower is said to have sprung up wherever Mary's foot touched the earth when she was on her way to visit her cousin, Elizabeth.

Three months after the angel appeared to tell her she would bear the son of God, Mary made the trip from Nazareth to the little village of Ain Karem in the mountains of Judea. There Elizabeth lived with her husband, Zechariah the priest. An angel had appeared to Zechariah, telling him his wife would at long last bear a child, and Mary went to be with Elizabeth. While she visited, she liked to spend time in the garden, meditating on her destiny. She touched a certain flower which grew there and it became very fragrant.

In a scene of the visitation from the fourteenth-century Prayerbook of Michelino de Besozzo, Mary and Elizabeth are surrounded by columbine florets. The columbine reflected the innocence of the Virgin Mary. An anonymous twelfth-century poem calls out:

> *Columbina per innocentiam…*
> Columbine because of her innocence
> *transplantavit in mente Virgini Filius hominis*
> He transplanted the God-man in the soul of the Virgin

The deep purple blooms also stood for the sorrow of Mary at the Cross, based on the relationship between the French name for the plant (ancolie) and the English word "melancholy" (*melancolie*).

The spurred flower resembles a little dove and came to symbolize the Holy Spirit. The name columbine comes from *columba*, the Latin word for dove. Since the curved petals also resemble an eagle, we have the botanical name, *aquilegia*, which comes from *aquila*, Latin for "eagle."

Early Flemish painters increased the number of petals from five to seven to represent the seven gifts of the Holy Spirit. Doves were placed above Mary in paintings, representing the seven gifts of the Holy Spirit.

In England doves were used to decorate the altar in Whitsun Week, the week following Pentecost Sunday, as the faithful made a connection between the dove, the Holy Spirit and Our Lady's Flower, the name they had given the columbine.

Sometimes the columbine symbolized the gifts of the spirit promised to the Messiah as in Bernardino Luini's sixteenth-century "Madonna in the Rose Arbour," where the child Jesus grasps the stem of columbine growing in a pot. In Hugo van der Goes's "Adoration of the Shepherds," a columbine with seven blossoms is placed in a vase before the infant Jesus.

Abbess Hildegard of Bingen in 1150 included the columbine in a list of wild plants known to her. During the Middle Ages it was an important medicinal herb and was one of the seven herbs used as a cure for the "pestilence." Albertus the Great, Dominican theologian and scientist, refers to the columbine in the pleasure garden described in his treatise, "On Vegetables and Plants," written around 1260.

This flower is one of more than one hundred species of plants and trees known in the Middle Ages and depicted in the Unicorn Tapestries, woven circa 1500 and full of Christian symbolism. The flowers in the tapestries are said to be more faithful to the actual flowers in nature than the botanical illustrations of the same period. The seven tapestries and a fantasy garden of about fifty species depicted in the tapestries are found at The Cloisters in New York City.

The columbine is found in the Mary Garden at the Episcopal Convent of the Transfiguration in Cincinnati, and at the Garden of Our Lady at the Knock Shrine in County Mayo.

*"Did I not see you
in the garden with him?"*

—JOHN 18:26

Our Lady's Bedstraw

Galium verum
Yellow Bedstraw, Our Lady's Bedstraw
(P)

∽ Meditation ∽

Unwelcomed at journey's end, lowly and poor—does no one care about the destiny of this woman with child and about the man who can provide only a cave-barn in this moment of need?

Mary, did you nevertheless see the gifts at hand: sweet sainfoin straw, the hollow trough, privacy? In every instance, let me see gift.

❧ Legend ❧

In Jesus' time, and into the sixteenth century, beds were made of straw. When Mary and Joseph arrived at the inn in Bethlehem they learned there was no room for them except in the stable where the cattle rested. There Joseph spread the dried straw and grasses which the innkeeper offered them, preparing a couch for Mary. Bedstraw, sainfoin, thyme and sweet woodruff were among the herbs used, and after Jesus' birth the dried grasses burst into flowers. Mary's bed was a "verdant mass of green, interspersed with tiny sweet-smelling flowerets," most noticeably the blossoms of yellow bedstraw.

It is told also that Mary herself lined the manger for the Infant and that the sainfoin began to bloom, circling Jesus' head with a wreath of pink clover-like flowers. The French called the sainfoin "Holy Hay."

Another legend tells of the white blossoms of bedstraw turning to gold with the radiance of Jesus at the hour in which he was born.

In the thirteenth century in Italy, the first Franciscan friars wrote many Christmas carols. The melody for the one which follows was used by Handel in his oratorio, "The Messiah." In English translation the carol begins:

> In Bethlehem is born the Holy Child
> On hay and straw in the winter wild;
> O, my heart is full of mirth
> At Jesus' birth.

By the sixteenth century the symbolism of Our Lady's Bedstraw was well-known. Joannes Bauhinus the Younger called it "*S. Mariae stramen*" or Saint Mary's Straw in "*De Plantis a divis Sanctisve nomen habentibus*" ("Plants Having Various Holy Names"), in Basel, Switzerland, in 1591. Early in the same century it grew in the St. Mary's Garden at Mailros (Melrose) Abbey in Scotland.

Bedstraw is seen in Piero di Cosimo's "Madonna Adoring the Child." A painting of "The Nativity" by Nicolas Poussin depicts the golden shower of the cradle grasses reflecting the golden rays surrounding the sleeping infant Jesus.

Writing early in the twentieth century, Sister Mary Francesca tells the story of the glow-worm, a tiny insect that watched Joseph spreading straw for Mary. Wanting to do something but unable to do much, the little worm found

> ....a tiny sprig of withered hay
> And climbed with it unto the manger high
> To help to make the bed on which he lay
> And "dropped my twig to join the rest."

The Child looked down and smiled
"On me, the lowliest of all things that move.
A ray of moonlight fell athwart His brow
And touched me too, as He put forth His hand
And blessed me. Therefore ever since that day
Glorious with light I sparkle through the land.

In medieval times bedstraw, thyme and other herbs were used as a "strewing herb" on floors of homes, churches, theaters and other public places because of their pleasant scent and medicinal properties. Dried bedstraw is still used to stuff mattresses. Manger herbs also include mints, especially pennyroyal, which was used to mask the odor of the animals and kill fleas. Mints were often called Our Lady's Mint.

Our Lady's Bedstraw is known as cradle grass in Sweden. White bedstraw (*Galium mollugo*) and creeping white thyme (*Thymus serpyllum*) are also called Mary's Bedstraw. Sainfoin (*Onobrychis vicifolia*) is known as Holy Clover or Holy Hay in France.

Known in Ireland as Mary's Bedstraw, yellow bedstraw is found near Mary's statue in the Garden of Our Lady at the Knock Shrine in County Mayo. Our Lady's Bedstraw grows in the herb gardens of the Mary Gardens at Annapolis, Maryland, and Portage, Michigan. Rosy thyme, also called Our Lady's Bedstraw, surrounds the statue of the Virgin in the Garden of Our Lady at Woods Hole. In the Mary Garden in Cincinnati, sweet woodruff is called Our Lady's Bedstraw.

"and she...laid him in a manger."

— LUKE 2:7

Carnation

Dianthus caryophyllus
Mary's Love of God and Divine Flower

(P)

☙ Meditation ☙

Carnation: smell of spice, color of our fleshiness, riotous wonder where angel choirs sing. Marvelous mystery of God among us. The word alone evokes the mystery: Word Made Flesh—Incarnation. The mighty God assumes our flesh.

With you, Mary, we sing Magnificat. Our souls magnify his name and all creation honors his birth.

⚭ Legend ⚭

A German legend says that the carnation bloomed on the night of Jesus' birth. The German peasants of the last century also told that the apple tree bloomed on Christmas Eve.

It was reported by Pope Innocent III that on the night of Jesus' birth, the Temple of Peace in Rome, housing the statue of Romulus, crumbled to the ground. The oracle of Apollo had declared that the statue and the temple would stand until the day when a virgin would give birth to a child. The church of Santa Maria Nuova now stands on the site of the former temple.

Another legend says that the carnation first appeared on earth on the day that Christ was crucified. Mary cried when she saw Jesus carrying the cross on the way to Calvary and the flowers sprang from her tears.

The carnation was considered an attribute of the Virgin Mary as early as the thirteenth century and was used as a simile for the Virgin Mary in German devotional poems of the time. In his *"Goldener Schmiede"* ("The Golden Forge") Konrad von Wurzburg called Mary a "fragrant carnation sprig." A recent analysis of the flowers in "The Virgin and Child in a Garland," attributed to Frans Yvens and Gerard Sehers, states the carnation evokes the perfume of the Virgin as well as the redemption.

The carnation also represented the Incarnation of Christ. The Blessed Virgin is depicted handing a carnation to the Christ Child in "Madonna and Child Enthroned with Four Angels" by Girolamo di Giovanni da Camerino, "Madonna and Child With a Carnation" by Bartolomeo Montagna and "Madonna and Child" by Leonardo da Vinci. A carnation appears at the feet of the Virgin Mary in Stefano da Verona's "Adoration of the Magi."

The carnation was sometimes substituted for roses and lilies in paintings of the assumption of the Virgin Mary and in some cases appeared alongside them. Three carnations are thought to represent roses in the central panel of a triptych of the Nativity, which depicts the "Adoration of the Shepherds," where they appear along with columbine, a lily, violets and iris. Known as the Portinari altarpiece because it was commissioned by Tommaso Portinari, an agent of the Medici in Bruges, the altarpiece was painted by Hugo van der Goes around 1476.

William the Conqueror is thought to have brought the carnation from Normandy to Britain in the eleventh century. It is also reported that carnations were imported to Europe in the late thirteenth century after Crusaders stricken with the plague in Tunis found that leaves of pinks mixed with wine helped control their fevers. They brought the plants to France where they were called *tunica.*

The blossoms were used to make crowns and wreaths by the Greeks and later the English, and were called "coronations." They were called gillyflowers or July-flowers, presumably because they bloomed in July. In the fifteenth century the name "carnation" (from "coronation") was given both to single (pinks) and double blooms (*Clove gillefloures*).

The plant's name *Dianthus* comes from the Greek words *dios* for "divine" and *anthos* meaning "flower." It came to mean "flower of God" and became associated with Mary.

Carnations grow in the Bonnefont Cloister herb garden, representative of monastic kitchen and infirmary gardens, and in the garden of the Trie Cloister at The Cloisters. More than fifty species of flowers, shrubs and trees depicted in seven fifteenth-century tapestries titled "The Hunt of the Unicorn" (which hang in The Cloisters) are found in the Trie Cloister garden. In medieval times the unicorn represented Christ, who was born of the Virgin Mary and raised up a horn of salvation.

The clove pink (*Dianthus plumarius*) is found in the shady Mary Garden of the Episcopal Convent of the Transfiguration in Cincinnati, where it is known as Virgin Pink.

"While they were there (in Bethlehem), the time came for her to deliver her child. And she gave birth to her firstborn son and wrapped him in bands of cloth, and laid him in a manger."

— LUKE 2:6-7

Christmas Rose

Helleborus niger
Holy Night Rose or Rose de Noel

(P)

⨀ Meditation ⨀

Angels and shepherds, kings and children; there is room for everyone in the Bethlehem cave. What desire in the human heart to give gifts to the beloved! I do not wish to stand before the child and his mother empty-handed. Like little Madelon in legend, I need to realize that the most precious gift I can give the tiny Christ Child is the gift of my love. So, angels, sweep away the coldness that covers my gift.

Mary, the Christmas rose with its soft ivory petals, nestled in lacy green leaves, blooms in the midst of winter—an astonishing and comforting sight during the dark, fruitless season. Sometimes my heart is as cold and hard as the winter ground. Warm me, and offer my heart to your Child.

❦ Legend ❦

On the night that Jesus was born a young shepherd girl named Madelon followed the other shepherds to Bethlehem to see the infant wrapped in swaddling clothes that the angel of the Lord had told them about. Her tender maiden heart was moved when she saw the infant laid in a manger, with straw for a bed, and the Holy Family struggling to keep warm in the cave. She wanted to offer something to comfort Mary and show her love for Jesus, but she was poor and had nothing to give.

The shepherds played a lullaby on their rustic pipes and offered a covering of fleece for the baby's bed. The wise men came bearing gifts of gold, frankincense and myrrh for Jesus.

Madelon stood nearby, quietly weeping because she had nothing for the baby. God saw her distress and sent the angel Gabriel to her. "Madelon, what makes you weep while you pray?" the angel asked.

"I weep because I have nothing to offer to the infant Jesus. If only I had some flowers to give him I should be happy, but it is winter, and the frost is on the ground and spring is far away. Good angel, I am most distraught," Madelon answered.

Gabriel took Madelon by the hand and led her out into the night and as they walked the cold seemed to disappear and they were surrounded by a bright, golden light. They paused and Gabriel touched the frozen earth with his staff. Immediately creamy white blossoms flushed with pink sprang up everywhere. The young maiden filled her arms with the flowers and ran to decorate Jesus' bed and the stable where Mary had borne him.

The story was told in mystery plays of medieval times. In another version the angel swooped down and with her wings swept off a blanket of snow, uncovering roses blooming at the girl's feet. Yet another version says that God sent the angel Gabriel to Madelon and after learning why she wept, the angel touched the earth with his staff and blossoms sprang up; she gathered them and decorated the cave where Jesus lay.

The French poet, Emile Blemont, ended his story of Madelon with this quatrain:

> Though thou art poor and hast no gold to bring,
> Though ice-bound earth no Heaven-sent flowers bestows,
> Yet give thy heart this Noel to thy King.
> This is the Legend of the Christmas Rose.

The rose was a medieval symbol of the Virgin Birth of Christ, as expressed by Dante: "Behold the Rose wherein the Divine Word was made incarnate."

Because in some areas it blooms at Christmastime, the Christmas rose became the symbol of the nativity. In High Dutch it was called "Christ's herbe" because it blooms about the time of Jesus' birth. The flowers are resistant to cold, blooming in February or March, and earlier if in a protected site or warmer climate.

It is told that at the very hour that Christ was born, when shepherds were watching their flocks through the night, an angel appeared, announcing the birth of the Savior and telling them where they would find him. It was customary for shepherds and others to stay awake during the nights of the summer and winter solstices, the longest and shortest nights of the year, and this was the night of the winter solstice.

The evergreen plant, native to southern Europe, was introduced by the Romans to England, possibly in the first century. It is found in the mostly shade Mary Garden at the Episcopal Convent of the Transfiguration in Cincinnati.

"In that region there were shepherds living in the fields, keeping watch over their flocks by night. Then an angel of the Lord stood before them, and the glory of the Lord shone around them."

— LUKE 2:8-9

Oxeye Daisy

Chrysanthemum leucanthemum

Mary's Star

(P)

∞ Meditation ∞

Things, persons, events are prophets pointing the way to God, are priests and people praising God. All created being is in some form a transparency of God. It remains for us to discern god-likeness in order to better understand the mystery of God made man.

Did you learn, Mary, to discern God's graces long before Bethlehem and the coming of your child? Did you long for him, seek him, serve him? Did you pluck the flower and bury your face in its petals, wondering at the majesty of his love? Did you ever imagine he would entrust himself to you? If only I could share your wisdom, as did the wise men who knelt down before the child in your arms.

❧ Legend ❧

On the night that Jesus was born the Magi, praying on a mountainside, saw a star appear in the form of a fair child. The child told them to go to Jerusalem, where they would find a newborn child.

When the wise men, following the star, reached the village of Bethlehem, they looked for a further sign. It was dark and everything was quiet and they did not know which house to enter. Suddenly King Melchior saw a strange white and gold flower that looked like the star that had led them to Bethlehem. As he bent to pick it, the door of a stable opened and he saw the Holy Family.

Another legend tells of golden yellow flowers blooming in front of the manger in Bethlehem, marking it for the wise men by their resemblance to the star shining in the sky above. It is said that after leading the wise men to Bethlehem, the star took root as a glorious golden chrysanthemum, marking the entrance to the manger.

The Magi are thought to have arrived in Bethlehem twelve days after Christmas, the day celebrated as the Feast of the Epiphany since the third century. Originally this day also marked the birth of Jesus, but when the feast of Christmas began to be celebrated in the fourth century, this day then commemorated the Baptism of Christ.

A legend found in *Collectanea et Flores*, a book from the eighth century ascribed to Saint Bede the Venerable, describes the Magi:

> The first was called Melchior; he was an old man, with white hair and long beard; he offered gold to the Lord as to his king. The second, Gaspar by name, young, beardless, of ruddy hue, offered to Jesus his gift of incense, the homage due to divinity. The third, of black complexion, with heavy beard, was called Baltasar; the myrrh he held in his hands prefigured the death of the Son of man.

One of the oldest legends about the wise men was told by Saint Gregory of Tours in 594 in his *Libri Miraculorum* ("Book of Miracles"). The people of Bethlehem were said to go to the Well of the Magi during Christmas week. Covering themselves and the opening of the well to shut out the light they would peer into the well. Only those who were pure of heart could see the star of Bethlehem moving slowly across the water in the well.

Legends about Mary have been traced back to the eleventh century, but their popularity began in the latter half of the twelfth century. Mystery plays also began to be performed about this time. A mystery play called "Office of the Star," a pageant about the Magi's visit on the Feast of the Epiphany, began as part of the liturgical service in the eleventh century, probably in France. After it degenerated to a boisterous affair, it was replaced by the "Feast of the Star," performed partly in church and partly outdoors, but not connected with the liturgy.

In Wales the oxeye daisy is known as "trembling star." In the nineteenth century in Mauritius one of two original species of this plant, *Chrysanthemum indicum*, was known as the Christmas flower because it bloomed in December. It was also called Mary's Flower of God, suggesting the divine flower, Christ, whom she bore.

Medieval Paradise Gardens often included a flowery mead. Oxeye daisies were interspersed with many other Mary-named herbs and flowers, among them rose campion, lavender, coral bells, forget-me-not and mints. Oxeye daisies were favored in garlands for decorating churches for feast days and other celebrations.

The flower has bright yellow centers with stark white ray-like petals and grows mostly on single stems. It's a familiar weed in the eastern United States and Europe. Perhaps for that reason it is not found in any of the known Mary Gardens. It can be seen in the Bonnefont Cloister herb garden at The Cloisters.

"On entering the house, they saw the child with Mary his mother; and they knelt down and paid him homage."

— MATTHEW 2:11

Star of Bethlehem

Ornithogalum umbellatum
Star of the Cross, Mary's Tears

(P)

⋘ Meditation ⋙

Stars radiate on the horizon, fields flower unexpectedly, wise strangers visit. Mary and Joseph, filled with wonder, marvel at the mystery of their mutual treasure, the child Jesus, who is God with them, Emmanuel. Do we not sense that love beyond all description has brought all these together in time and place, in a plan far vaster than the miracles of flowers in the field and endless eons of the night?

Mary, what an incredible thing that you may hold the center of the universe to your breast! Could we hold him for a little while? Perhaps in this child's embrace we, too, will behold his glory and find our God as we have never before found him. Perhaps his cheek touching ours will reveal to us our reason for existence and we will begin to believe, as he did, in the possibility of a Father God's eternal love, defying the boundaries of space and limits of time, with but one intent: after the journey, to bring us home.

❧ Legend ❧

The flower is said to resemble the star of the east that pointed to the birth-place of Jesus. The star shone brightly in the night and guided the shepherds to the place where the newborn Jesus lay, then broke into little pieces, scattering white blossoms everywhere.

Another legend says that after it directed the Magi to Jesus, having served its purpose, the star burst forth like a meteor, scattering little pieces over the fields and bursting into flowers. Saint Joseph then gathered an armful of the lilies and filled Mary's lap with them, saying, "See the Star of the East has fallen and borne fruit in kind."

It is also told that after many years had passed the wise men were visited by Saint Thomas the apostle, who instructed them in Christianity and baptized them. Later, after they were ordained to the priesthood and then made bishops, the star of Bethlehem appeared to them once more, reuniting them at the end of their lives.

In Germany and England the flower is known as the Star of Bethlehem but in France and Italy the blossoms are known as Mary's Tears. The fallen white petals resemble tears, and it is said that when Mary held up the divine Child to receive the homage of the wise men, she wept at the contrast of the poverty of the manger in the cattle shed and the majesty of her son. The delicate little flowers sprang up wherever her tears fell.

The plant grows abundantly in Judea and is thought to have been brought to Europe by pilgrims and Crusaders. Beginning at the end of the fourteenth century and lasting until the Reformation in the sixteenth century, "Star Carols," a simplified form of older Epiphany plays, told the story of the Magi. Young people went from house to house on January 6, the Feast of Epiphany, carrying a pole with the "Star of Bethlehem" and impersonating the Magi. They sang of the adventures of their journey and wished all a happy and holy Christmas. One song began with the words:

> We are the three Kings with our star,
> We bring you a story from lands afar...

This custom was widespread in England, Holland, France, Austria and Germany and was still practiced in Austria, Bavaria and the Slavic countries early in this century.

"Star-floures," or stars of Bethlehem, were known in England in the sixteenth century and are mentioned in Gerard's *Herbal* as referring to "sundry kindes of wilde field Onions."

In nineteenth-century England the greater stitchwort or stellary was known as the native star of Bethlehem. Saint-John's-Wort was known as the Bethlehem or Jerusalem star and in North America the aster was called the Christmas starwort or the daisy of December. Use of the poinsettia at Christmastime began because the red bracts resembled the flaming Star of Bethlehem.

The star of Bethlehem's blossom is a small, fragrant, satiny white flower, green-striped white on the outside, appearing in clusters in the spring. It is found in the Mary Garden of the Episcopal Convent of the Transfiguration in Cincinnati, where it is called Mary's Tears.

*"We observed his star
at its rising,
and have come to
pay him homage."*

— MATTHEW 2:2

Thistle

Carduus benedictus, Carduus marianus,
Cnicus benedictus, and *Silybum marianum*
Our Lady's Thistle, Virgin Mary's Thistle,
Blessed Thistle and Milk Thistle

(P)

Meditation

Even the thistle is blessed and given its due right to exist. Left in the wild, the thistle has a beauty all its own: feather softness, scarlet purple crown, silver-lined spike leaves. But the deep-rooted thistle can destroy our garden, torment us, and draw blood when we touch it. The persistent sting of the thistle in our gardens can be a symbol for us of what we humans can do in the deep darkness of our hearts and backbiting blindness of our minds.

Mary, how do we handle the thistles of our lives? How do we endure the thistle spines that pierce even our protective shields? How do we bear the stings that fester and spread poison through the body? Only the milk of mercy can transform all pain and lead to the healing of salvation.

∽ Legend ∽

The white veins traced on the leaves of the plant are said to be from the drops of Mary's milk falling on them when the Blessed Mother moved her baby from her breast after feeding him.

It is said that after Jesus' birth, the Holy Family moved from the stable at the inn to a grotto where they had more privacy. Known as the Milk Grotto, it was remarkable for the purity of its limestone which was said to have become flawless after some drops from Mary's breast fell on its surface. Pieces of limestone from the grotto, preserved as relics, were found with the label "*Lac Beatae Mariae*" (Milk of the Blessed Mary) in old churches in England in the nineteenth century.

The thistle was connected with the Virgin Mary from medieval times. Early botanists called the plant *Lac Beatae Mariae* and it became associated with Mary in every country where it was found, from Italy to Sweden. In France the plant was known as *Chardon de Notre Dame*, Our Lady's Thistle.

In 1539 Joannes Ammonius Agricola called the white thistle "S. Mary's Thistle" in his "*Medicinae Herbariae Libri Duo*":

Carduus albus	White thistle
Recentiores Carduum	More recently called
Mariae nominant	Mary's Thistles

At the end of the sixteenth century the English botanist Gerard wrote of the blessed thistle, called *Carduus benedictus*, which "brings forth floures consisting of many whitish threds."

Thistle grew in St. Mary's garden at Melrose Abbey in Scotland in the early sixteenth century, which had "as many plants with white flowers as could be obtained, for the white was symbolic of (Mary's) purity and holiness."

More than twenty thorny plants are mentioned in the Bible, and from seventy to one hundred twenty kinds of thistles are said to grow in Israel. Thistle florets may be white, yellow or purple.

Pilgrims to the Holy Land told of seeing thistles of many kinds bearing foliage of a milk-stained grain as they walked on sacred soil. Their listeners would connect the plants with Mary's name, calling them Virgin Mary's milk thistle or blessed thistle.

Thistle became the emblem for the order of knighthood begun in 1370 by Louis, Duke of Bourbon; he called the order "Our Lady of the Thistle."

The bright purple blossoms of the thistle were said to grace our Lady's path when she went to visit Elizabeth, and the soft down of the spent blooms were ready in August to make a pillow for Mary's tomb. Thistledown was a symbol of the annunciation because of its graceful movement in the air. It is found in a scene of the annunciation from a sixteenth-century French *Book of Hours*.

Several other plants also hold the tradition that Mary's milk fell on them. The gray powdery lichen attached to the roots of polypody ferns is said to have originated from the Blessed Mother's milk falling on earth and the fern springing from the stained soil. This fern, known as Mary's Fern, was called *Marien-Milch* in Germany and *Marie bregne* (Mary's milk) in France.

Blessed thistle is found in the Bonnefont Cloister herb garden and the Trie Cloister garden at The Cloisters.

"Thorn and thistle shall grow up
on their altars.
They shall say to the mountains,
Cover us,
and to the hills, Fall on us."

— HOSEA 10:8

Snowdrop

Galanthus nivalis
The Flower of the Purification,
Fair Maid of February, Candlemas Bells

(P)

∽ Meditation ∼

The Feast of the Presentation of the Lord in the Temple is a constant reminder that Jesus subjected himself to the law. Those closest to him, Mary and Joseph, followed the command of this law, brought him to the temple of their faith, and through sacrifice bought him back in order to provide for him in the nest of a human family.

Every family is like a garden that needs to be tended well; every person belongs in some way to a family. There are roles to fulfill and sacrifices to be made. Joseph, Mary, Jesus give wholeness to the families we call our own, even when our hearts experience brokenness.

⚮ Legend ⚮

The snowdrop is said to have bloomed on February 2, when Mary took Jesus to the Temple to present him to God. According to the law of Moses, Mary, like every Jewish mother, was excluded from public worship in the temple for forty days after giving birth. At the end of that time she was to come to the temple and make an offering, purifying herself from ritual uncleanness. She would also present her son to God. February 2, forty days after Christ's birth, thus became known as the Feast of the Purification, or the Feast of the Presentation of Jesus.

In 701 Pope Sergius I directed that a procession with candles begin the celebration of the Feast of the Purification, as well as three other feasts of Mary: the annunciation, assumption and nativity of Mary. On February 2, which then became known also as Candlemas Day, the procession was a symbol of the journey of Mary, Joseph, Simon and Anna to the Temple when they presented the Child Jesus. Lighted candles were carried as if to say, "Most blessed Virgin, thou has no need of purification, on the contrary, thou art all light and all purity."

Another reason given for the holding of lighted candles by the faithful is to recall the prophecy of Simon at the time of the Presentation of Jesus in the Temple that Jesus was to be a "light for revelation to the Gentiles." The twinkling of lights in the church reminded one early English writer of the drooping white snowdrops dotting the meadows and woods.

In Germany the feast is called *Lichtmess*, in Spain *Candelas* and in Italy it is *Candelora*. The French call it *Chandeleur*. The practice of blessing the candles began at the end of the eighth century in the Carolingian Empire. Later in England the custom began of women carrying a lighted candle at the ceremony of their "churching" or blessing after childbirth.

In a poem called "An Early Calendar of English Flowers" we find these lines:

> The Snowdrop, purest white arraie,
> First rears her hede on Candlemas daie.

In the early sixteenth century the monks at Melrose Abbey in Scotland, dedicated to Mary, believed that the snowdrop, which grew in the Mary Garden there, bloomed on February 2 in memory of the Virgin Mary presenting her child Jesus to the temple.

The pure white flower became an emblem of Our Lady's purity. In Italy and other countries the statue of Our Lady was removed from the altar on February 2 and snowdrops were strewn in its place.

These lines from a late nineteenth-century poem tell of the flower's symbolism:

Sweet flowers of Our Lady, sweet Candlemas Bells!
I listen and listen—a mystery dwells
In your white drooping petals, my Candlemas Bells.

In England it is said that monks visiting from Italy in the first century brought the flower with them, also that monks cultivated the plant which they found in the damp woodlands of the north country and Herefordshire. They grew the plant in monastery gardens for use on Candlemas Day and other feast days of Mary, calling the flowers Candlemas Bells. The plant appears in paintings of medieval Paradise Gardens.

The leaves of the plant resemble miniature versions of iris "sword" foliage, an association with the sorrowful prophecy of Simon: "and a sword will pierce your own soul too."

The generic name, *galanthus*, comes from the Greek and means "milk flower"; *nivalis* is Latin and means "of the snow." The white flowers have greenish stripes on the petals. It is distinguished from the snowflake (*Leucojum aestivum*) which was called *Zomerzot-jes* in Holland because it was foolish enough to wait until early summer to bloom.

The plant is found in Mary Gardens in Woods Hole; Portage, Michigan; and Cincinnati. It also grows in the Garden of Our Lady at Knock in Ireland. The snowdrop, as well as the snowflake, grows in the garth or enclosed garden of the Cuxa Cloister at The Cloisters.

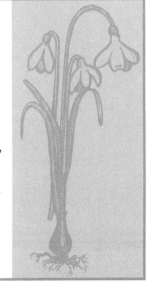

"When the time came for their purification according to the law of Moses, they brought him up to Jerusalem to present him to the Lord.... Then Simeon blessed them and said to his mother Mary, 'This child is destined for the falling and the rising of many in Israel, and to be a sign that will be opposed so that the inner thoughts of many will be revealed— and a sword will pierce your own soul too.'"

— LUKE 2:22, 34-35

Jerusalem Cowslip

Pulmonaria officinalis
Spotted Lungwort, Spotted Cowslip of Jerusalem,
Mary's Tears, Virgin Mary's Tears
(P)

⚬ Meditation ⚬

No matter what color, blue eyes or brown eyes—or green or gray—all can weep bitterly. When we plan and plant our garden, none of us can escape the plough and hoe, the sickle and pike. Gardening, much like birthing, wrenches life from life, yet joy—not death—is our final purpose for the garden.

Faithful woman under the cross, share your hours of sorrow with us. Let us share ours with you. Let us together hope for the healing this pain will bring.

❧ Legend ❧

Several legends relate to Mary traveling to Jerusalem to present Jesus in the temple. It was a long journey from Nazareth and she sat down at the edge of the road to nurse her son. The spotted cowslip was growing at her feet and its blooms turned blue as they reflected the blue of the Blessed Mother's eyes. Her eyes filled with tears as she thought of the poverty and future suffering of her child, and the buds of the flowers grew pink as her eyes reddened from weeping. As she moved the infant Jesus from her breast a few drops of her milk fell on the plant, spotting the leaves which have ever since borne the white markings of her milk.

In another version, Mary sat down to nurse Jesus on her way out of Jerusalem, after presenting Jesus in the temple. The plant at her feet caught the blue of her eyes but the blossoms turned pink as Mary's eyes reddened from weeping as she remembered the sorrowful prophecy of Simon and reflected on the suffering predicted for her son.

Other legends tell that at the foot of the cross on Calvary Mary's eyes were as blue as the fully opened blossoms, but her eyelids were as red as the buds from crying. The spots on the leaves are the marks of the tears Mary shed at the crucifixion.

It is reported that in Dorset, England, the cottagers liked to have spotted lungwort in their gardens and called it "Maery's Tears." There the mothers told their children the story of Mary and her child as they pointed to the leaves and flowers of the plant.

The Elizabethan botanist, Gerard, called *Pulmonaria* the spotted cowslip of Jerusalem. In medieval times the plant was dedicated to Our Lady throughout England and northern Europe. In England it was called the Virgin Mary's Milkdrops or Tears, the Virgin Mary's Cowslip or honeysuckle and the cowslip of Bethlehem. In Wales it was *Llaeth bron Mair* or Mary's Breast Milk. In France and Belgium it was called *L'herbe au lait de Notre Dame*, the herb of Our Lady's Milk. In Germany and Holland it was *Unser lieben Frauen Melchkraut*, and in Italy it was known as *Erba della Madonna*, herb of the Madonna.

The cowslip is found in "The Garden of Paradise," painted by a master from the Upper Rhine in Germany in the early fifteenth century. This painting is noted for the symbolism of the many flowers depicted. Among the more than eighteen flowers represented are these associated with Mary through naming or legend: rose campion, cowslip, purple flag iris, Madonna Lily, lily of the valley, rose, sage, snowdrop, strawberry and violet.

The Marian names of the cowslip have survived even to this day. Botanical guides list several species of *Pulmonaria*—perennial herbs of Europe and Asia.

The species *officinalis* is called Jerusalem cowslip or Jerusalem sage. One variety is known as *Immaculata*. The species *saccharata* is called Bethlehem sage. Spiderwort, *Tradescantia virginiana*, native to North and South America, is called widow's tears and is also known as Our Lady's Tears.

Spiderwort grows in Mary Gardens in Annapolis, Portage and Woods Hole, where it is known variously as Our Lady's Tears, Lady's Tears and The Virgin's Tears.

*"I have heard your prayer,
I have seen your tears;
indeed I will heal you."*

— 2 KINGS 20:5

Clematis

Clematis vitalba

Virgin's Bower

(P)

⟶ Meditation ⟵

We know our clematis, intertwining porch and trellis with blossoms white or purple. We look with pride at its beauty. We marvel at the mantle it creates.

Mary, when you looked into your child's face, did you see all the loveliness of the universe—everything beautiful, holy and good? Yet here you were, on the flight to Egypt to save his life. Were you overwhelmed with his mystery and the fullness of your love for him? Or, did you wonder what bitter pain awaited him, as it somehow does for each of us, and hide him in the folds of your mantle? Like the clematis did for you, become a refuge for us.

⌒ Legend ⌒

According to a German legend, wild clematis sheltered Mary and Jesus on their flight into Egypt. After the wise men left the Holy Family, returning to their country by a different route so as to avoid King Herod, an angel appeared in a dream to Joseph. The angel told him, "Get up, take the child and his mother, and flee to Egypt, and remain there until I tell you; for Herod is about to search for the child, to destroy him" (Matthew 2:13). The Holy Family left Jerusalem that night, traveling in the dark. It is thought that they journeyed across the hill country of Judea to Hebron, then to the coast and south into Egypt. The trip, partly through desert, may have taken six to seven weeks.

Clematis, growing among the hedgerows along the road and vining from twenty to thirty feet, provided shelter for the Holy Family from the sun during the day and the cold during the night. It blooms in May and June, its lovely white blossoms giving forth a sweet fragrance.

Another legend says that angels were sent to guide the Holy Family, to watch over them by day, pitch a tent for them each night and refresh them with celestial fruit and flowers. Date trees lowered their branches so that the famished pilgrims could eat, and wells sprang up from the desert to slake their thirst.

In the British Isles the plant was called "traveler's joy," because its pleasant vanilla scent enchanted numerous foot travelers. It became known as Our Lady's Flower, as recorded in 1810 by Sir Walter Scott in "The Lady of the Lake":

> ...And clematis, that favored flower,
> Which boasts the name of Virgin's flower.

In late summer the feathery seed heads of the plant begin to blow. The flower continued to be associated with Mary, as seen in this couplet from "An Early Calendar of English Flowers":

> When Mary left us here below
> The Virgin's bower is full in blow.

Wild clematis grew along the roads of England during the time of the Roman occupation. During the Middle Ages it was used for "well-dressing," the custom of decorating wells with ten foot high pictures fashioned with flowers and greens to depict religious themes. Many of the wells had been dedicated to Mary in early Christian times and were blessed in annual ceremonies.

The most famous well-dressing ceremonies are held in Tissington, where it is said that in the mid-fourteenth century the residents escaped the Black Death because of the purity of the water, also that the five wells continued to supply water during the six-month-long drought of 1615. The custom continues in Tissington, where on Ascension Day a thanksgiving service is held at the parish church, following which the clergy, choir and parishioners process to bless each of the five wells.

The vine is found throughout Europe, in western Asia and North America. It grows in Mary Gardens in Annapolis, Maryland; Woods Hole, Massachusetts; and Portage, Michigan.

*"They shall again live
beneath my shadow,
they shall flourish as a garden;
they shall blossom like the vine,
their fragrance shall be like
the wine of Lebanon."*

— HOSEA 14:7

Rosemary

Rosemarinus officinalis
Arbor Sanctae Maria
Saint Mary's Tree

(P)

❧ Meditation ❧

A fragrant oil, useful for perfumes and fine cooking—the rosemary. The tiniest drop of oil will spread through the pages of a book and on a garment, to my amazement. I do my best to remove the stain, in vain. The sweet fragrance haunts me as I walk past my rosemary in the twilight. Words, too, can be balm, blessing and blame. Once spoken, they echo endlessly and penetrate every surface.

Mary, the last words I find attributed to you in the sacred texts are like the rosemary, sweet and irresistible: "Do whatever he tells you!" Remind the Lord for me to fill my empty wineskin with the joy of his Spirit.

✂ Legend ✂

The rosemary bush gave shelter to the Holy Family during the flight into Egypt. After Herod, king of Judea, heard about Jesus' birth and commanded his soldiers to kill all male infants under the age of two, Mary and Joseph fled Bethlehem with the infant Jesus, traveling to Egypt to escape the soldiers.

Rosemary is one of several bushes said to have sheltered the Holy Family, the others are clematis and juniper. It is one of the first plants to flower in spring.

The Holy Family is said to have encountered robber bands of nomadic Arabs, and tradition holds that the gypsies were a band of roaming marauders who were doomed to wander forever after they refused to shelter the Holy Family.

It is told that Mary hung the linens of the Holy Child on the rosemary bush to dry, and afterwards it became aromatic and evergreen, with little blue flowers springing up from its branches. The following was found in a small English book, *Our Ladye's Garlande*, published early in this century:

> Rosemary
> Rose of the World and Mary's Son,
> Son of the Maid who when day was done
> Washed the shift of her little One
> Singing, O Rose of Mary

From Melrose Abbey in Scotland comes the legend that after a shower Mary threw her blue cloak to dry over the rosemary bush and the white flowers turned blue in her honor. The abbey, originally known as Mailros, after Mary, was founded in 1136 and dedicated to the Virgin Mary by King David. In the early fifteenth century rosemary grew in a village near the abbey, according to a legend about David, a young boy who lived in the village.

David longed to become a monk but could not read or write. He knew how to make seeds grow in any kind of soil and his plants were always the first to grow. When he learned about Saint Fiacre, patron saint of flowers, David decided to grow the most beautiful flowers and serve the Lord as Saint Fiacre had done. He was devoted to the Virgin Mary and would bring armloads of flowers to the little village church to honor her.

One day one of the monks saw the boy cutting branches of the most luxuriant rosemary and carrying it toward the church. He followed David and found him praying before the shrine of the Virgin Mary. When the friar complimented the boy on his beautiful gift to Mary, David found the courage to confide his dream of joining the monks at the abbey. The monk told him he could come to live at the abbey where he would learn to read and write, and that he would be allowed to serve God with his gift of growing beautiful plants.

David went to the abbey, where he was given the job of tending the vegetables and flowers in St. Mary's Garden. He filled the monastery church, which until then had been decorated only by stone carvings, with masses of flowers. These lines from Sir Walter Scott bear witness to David's work:

> Spreading herbs, and flowerets bright
> Glistened with dew of night,
> Nor herb nor floweret glisten'd there
> But it was carved in the cloister arches as fair.

Shakespeare's Ophelia says "There's rosemary, that's for remembrance" (*Hamlet*, IV:v) Rosemary was known for remembrance of Mary, the Mystic Rose, the Rose of Sharon, and was considered a symbol of Mary's faithfulness.

The herb appears in plant lists of Palladius (c. 380), Charlemagne (c. 800) and in the Saint Gall plan (c. 820). It was imported to England from southern Europe in the fifteenth century, probably by monks who were the botanists of that time. It was said to grow up to three or four cubits (seven feet) in France, Spain and other hot countries, was used for hedges in the gardens of Italy and England and kept in pots in colder climates.

In Spain the plant is called "Romero," the pilgrim's flower. It is found in Our Lady's Garden in Woods Hole.

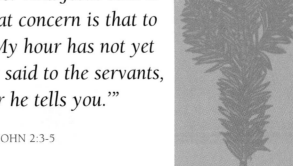

"When the wine gave out, the mother of Jesus said to him, 'They have no wine.' And Jesus said to her, 'Woman, what concern is that to you and to me? My hour has not yet come!' His mother said to the servants, 'Do whatever he tells you.'"

— JOHN 2:3-5

Juniper

Juniperis
The Madonna's Juniper Bush

(P)

❧ Meditation ❧

Our garden of life includes both blessing and despair. We marvel that the two can go hand in hand. Just as we note the splendor of our gardens, we also note the toil and sweat it takes over the years to establish a good garden. Ezekiel 31 compares the glory of Egypt to a wonderful garden. But Egypt worked hard to make a land where junipers can thrive.

Mary, you, Joseph and the Child would live there for a while. Did you hear the Scriptures and remember the story of your people in the nation that gave you shelter, the Egypt of blessing and the Egypt of despair? Sometimes I wonder how you mastered life in the desert. Teach me.

∽ Legend ∞

In Sicily, it is told that the juniper tree saved the life of Mary and the infant Jesus during their flight into Egypt. As the soldiers pursued them, the Holy Family passed by fields of peas and flax and thickets of various shrubs. The crackling and rustling sounds of the plants alarmed Mary, and it seemed as if the soldiers were almost upon them.

The Madonna's Juniper Bush, as it is known in Sicily, was growing nearby and opened up its thick branches to enclose the Holy Family, hiding them until Herod's men had passed by. The inside of the large bush became a soft bed, sheltering the fleeing family, while needles on the outside branches grew prickly as spears. Herod's soldiers could not penetrate the spiky branches of the juniper and passed the family by.

The Virgin Mary hid with Jesus under various plants and trees as Herod's soldiers sought them, and it is said that these plants received her blessing in return for their shelter. The juniper, which often grows to twenty feet in height in warm climates, was invested with the special power of putting to flight the spirits of evil. It became a sanctuary for animals in the woods and a sacred presence in homes and on altars, a reminder that it had protected the Holy Child. In France, Germany, Italy and Switzerland, juniper boughs were hung in stables and barns and near the crucifix in homes.

In another legend, it is said that as Herod's soldiers were in pursuit, Jesus and his parents passed a field where a man was sowing corn. Mary said to the farmer, "If anyone asks you whether we have passed this way, you shall answer: 'Such persons passed this way when I was sowing this grain.'" The Blessed Mother was too good and too wise to save her son by asking the man to tell a lie, so by the power of the infant Jesus the seed sprang up overnight and was ready for harvesting the next morning. When Herod's officers arrived at the field they found a man reaping grain. They inquired of him, "Have you seen an old man with a woman and a child traveling this way?" The man in truth replied, "Yes, when I was sowing this seed." It is said that Herod's soldiers turned back and ended their pursuit of the Holy Family.

In another version, possibly from England, Mary said to the peasant, "God be with thee, my good man! As soon as thou hast sown take thy sickle and reap." Then as soon as he had finished scattering seed at one end of the field it had ripened at the other end. When the soldiers came and asked when he had seen the family in flight, he replied, "Not long ago; just when I was sowing this wheat." The soldiers said, "That must have been twelve weeks ago," and turned back, thinking they could not overtake the fugitives.

The Magyars believed that each kernel of wheat, when split, would show the imprint of the Madonna and Child. In France it is said that Saint Amadour, who was Zaccheus of the Gospel, owned the field where the grain grew so miraculously.

A painting by Hans Memling, *"Die Sieben Freuden Maria"* ("The Seven Joys of Mary"), includes in the background the flight into Egypt, showing men cutting and reaping corn, while Herod's men pursue the Holy Family. The legend is also depicted in the fresco by Pinturicchio in St. Onofrio's Church in Rome.

The juniper mentioned in the Bible is thought to be *Genista raetum*, called white broom or juniper bush in Palestine, which produces a straggly plant not casting much shade. Juniper grew around Nineveh in 710 B.C. The common juniper is mentioned in the first European herbal, *De Materia Medica*, by a first-century Greek physician named Dioscorides. In the Middle Ages it was used in gardens with other scented herbs. An ancient Latin meaning for *juniper* is "forever young."

Juniper grows in Mary Gardens in Dayton, Ohio, St. Catherine's in Michigan and Knock, Ireland. It is found in the herb garden of the Bonnefont Cloister in New York.

"So when the plants came up and bore grain, then the weeds appeared as well.... 'Let both of them grow together until the harvest; and at harvest time I will tell the reapers, Collect the weeds first and bind them in bundles to be burned, but gather the wheat into my barn.'"

— MATTHEW 13:26, 30

Germander Speedwell

Veronica chamaedrys
Our Lady's Resting Place

(P)

∞ Meditation ∞

Rest restores vigor, even to a garden. No matter what the burden, once we have rested, hope springs fresh in the human heart and the world looks new. There are many ways to rest. Our gardens provide hidden corners where we can hide away. Just to watch the butterfly avoid the dewdrop can be a moment of rest.

Mary, what were your thoughts when you rested? Did you ponder, did you savor, was yours a resting in prayer—that is, a gentle speaking with the God of life within you, overshadowing you, and resting in your arms? Did you find refreshment in your quiet dialogue of love? Teach me how to rest!

Legend

In Europe the plant was known as Our Lady's Resting Place, after a legend that its blossoms marked each spot where the Blessed Mother rested during the flight into Egypt. In the Zillerthal area of Switzerland it was called *Unser lieben Frauen Rast*, or Our Dear Lady's Resting Place.

The journey from Judea to Egypt was long, about four hundred miles, through hill-country and desert, and perilous. Herod's men were looking for the Holy Family, and bands of robbers as well as wild animals posed many threats.

In Roman folklore it was told that one day while the Holy Family hurried to Egypt, the Madonna was carrying her baby through a field of vetch. The stalks of the plant rustled and Mary thought robbers were coming to kill her child. She turned and sent a malediction over the field and immediately the plants withered and fell to the ground and she could see that no one was hiding there. Assured that her son was safe, she sent a benediction over the field and the *Lupinus* (vetch) stood up straight and tall again, abundant and lush. Vetch is known as Flight to Egypt.

Germander became associated with long journeys in the British Isles, where travelers carried the blossoms to keep them safe on the route. In Ireland it was sewn into the clothes of travelers to keep them free from accidents.

The plant was well-known in medieval Europe. It first appears in a Latin poem, *De Viribus Herbarum*, written in 1050 by Macer Floridus, believed to be the pen name of French physician and herbalist Odo Magdunensis. In 1150 Abbess Hildegard of Bingen included it in her listing of plants known to her, in the category of wild plants with vernacular names. It was popular in the Germanic countries and appears in poems by the legendary minnesinger and lyric poet Tannhauser, in about 1240, as well as in a poem by Swiss Johans Hadloub, written about 1300. Tannhauser wrote:

> There stood violet and clover,
> Summer sprouts, germander,
> There were crocus,
> Flag iris found I there, lilies and roses.

In sixteenth-century England germander was one of the sweet-smelling herbs used for strewing floors of homes, theaters and churches. Along with basil, lavender and sage it was included in a 1573 list of twenty-one herbs to be planted for strewing use.

Germander was popular in medieval Paradise Gardens and was one of the low-growing plants used to make knots, or patterns, in gardens. Francesco

Colonna, a Dominican monk who wrote under the name Poliphilus about 1467, lists germander, rue, lavender, thyme and cat thyme as the principal herbs for the making of knots. His allegorical romance *Hypnerotomachia* describes imaginary gardens considered to be the forerunner of Italian Renaissance gardens. Meadows, called flowery medes, marble basins and fish ponds, latticework enclosures and trellises, classical colonnades and knot gardens were described, along with the flowers and herbs to be planted therein.

Other varieties of veronica are known as Lady's Faith (*Veronica maritima*) and Lady's Plant (*Veronica officinalis*), and two varieties of germander have Mary names: Lady's Little Flower (*Teucrium chamaedrys*) and Mary's Plant (*Teucrium polium*). While they belong to different families, veronica and germander are similar in that both are low-growing herbs or shrubs with stems up to eighteen inches and flowers less than one inch. Blossoms may be white, blue, rose or purple. Germander blooms in early spring and veronica in late spring.

Veronica speedwell is found in the Mary Garden at Annapolis and germander speedwell at Woods Hole. Several varieties grow in the garth garden of the Cuxa Cloister and the Bonnefont Cloister herb garden at The Cloisters.

"My heart is in anguish within me,
the terrors of death have fallen upon me....
And I say, 'O that I had wings like a dove!
I would fly away and be at rest;
truly, I would flee far away;
I would lodge in the wilderness.'"

— PSALM 55:4, 6-7

Rose of Jericho

Anastatica hierochuntica
Rose of the Virgin,
Holy Night Rose and Mary's Rose

(A)

∞ Meditation ∞

Legends abound concerning the flight cross the desert. Perhaps the mystery of the desert parallels the mystery of this couple fleeing persecution. The arid, windswept steppe can blossom overnight into a sea of Jericho roses, if once nourished by rainfall.

But it is this family which intrigues us. We first believe we cannot know much about them, yet if we stop to ponder the scriptural images—like this journey from Bethlehem to Egypt—we do indeed find scenes to describe them in the culture of their own time and nation. In just a few scenes Luke describes the Holy Family engaged in homemaking, carpentry, worship and celebration. These can give us insight about Jesus' growth in wisdom under the care of Joseph and Mary.

Holy couple, nurse us with your wisdom, nourish us with your pondering insight. Mary, Joseph, did you ever come to fully understand him? Will we? What love! O what enduring love!

❧ Legend ❧

It is told that the rose of Jericho sprang up to mark the spot at each place where the Holy Family rested during their flight to Egypt.

This plant, which looks like a dried-up ball of twigs when dormant, would have been found rolling across the desert sands as the Holy Family made its way to Egypt. After the plant blooms and its leaves wither and fall off, the stems curl up forming a ball with the roots, which separate from the soil. The rough sphere rolls across the desert sands, blown by the winds, until it reaches a damp place or winter rains moisten it. Then the globular mass unfolds, sheds its seeds and germinates, growing and producing small white blossoms.

The name, rose of Jericho, comes from the title given to Mary from the book of Sirach: "I grew tall...like rosebushes in Jericho." Some say it first blossomed the night of Jesus' birth. Legends told of the plant first blooming at the nativity, closing at the crucifixion and reviving again at Easter. Others said that it opened for all the feasts of Mary. It was called the resurrection plant because of the rapidity with which it comes to life and blooms in the desert after being given moisture.

Egypt was a customary place of refuge for the Jews and the traditions of the early Church told of several places in Egypt where the Holy Family stopped to rest before settling in one of the Jewish communities, possibly near Alexandria. Their first stop is said to have been at Heliopolis, near modern-day Cairo, where they went from door to door begging for food and water. The refugees did not receive the help they sought, so they left the city by the southern gate, and traveled to the nearby village of Matariyeh, or Matarea. There they rested in a grove of sycamores.

As Mary prayed for water to quench their thirst, a fountain miraculously sprang up nearby. Some say a well had already existed there, but the water had been brackish; the waters that now flowed were pure and untainted. The well still exists and is known as the Fountain of Mary. It is represented in scenes of the Holy Family resting during the flight into Egypt by Correggio, Baroccio and Domenichino. In a painting by Correggio, called the "*Madonna della Scodella*" ("Madonna of the Bowl"), Mary dips a bowl into a rushing stream.

For hundreds of years an old sycamore tree which leaned to one side because part of its trunk had decayed marked the spot where the Holy Family rested. It was known as the Virgin's Tree and may still grow there. J. L. Burckhardt, Egyptian student and traveler, wrote, "Since the Egyptian Sycamore, among various other trees, will live many thousand years, there is nothing absurd in the supposition that the Virgin may have sat with the Infant Saviour under the shade of this noble trunk."

Seventeenth-century travelers described the old tree, and in 1730 two men who saw it were convinced that it was the same tree as was honored in the second century.

The area enclosing the well and tree of the Holy Family is known as the Garden of Balsam. Early Christians believed that the sacred shrub, known from biblical days, sprang up in places in the garden where Mary bathed Jesus or washed his garments. The Nile flooded and destroyed the last balsam bush in 1615.

A fifteenth-century woodcut titled "Mary Washing the Child's Napkin" is accompanied by the legend that as "Mary and Joseph came with their Child to a garden in Babylonia, which had seven springs, there Mary washed the napkin of her dear Child in the spring." The print, from a Strasbourg book of 1494, was found in a collection of medieval woodcuts.

The rose of Jericho, native to the deserts of Arabia, Syria and Algeria, was brought to Europe by the Crusaders. In Germany and Switzerland it is known as *Marienrose*, in Italy as *Rose de la Madona*, in France as *Rose de Marie* and in Bohemia as *Ruze Panny Marie*. In Italy the annual sunflower (*Helianthus annuus*) is also known as the rose of Jericho. In the United States, the resurrection plant (*Selaginella lepidophylla*) is known as the rose of Jericho or desert rose. The plant is not found in Mary Gardens or cloister gardens.

*"Wisdom...grew tall
like a palm tree in Engedi,
and like rosebushes in Jericho."*

— SIRACH 24:1, 14

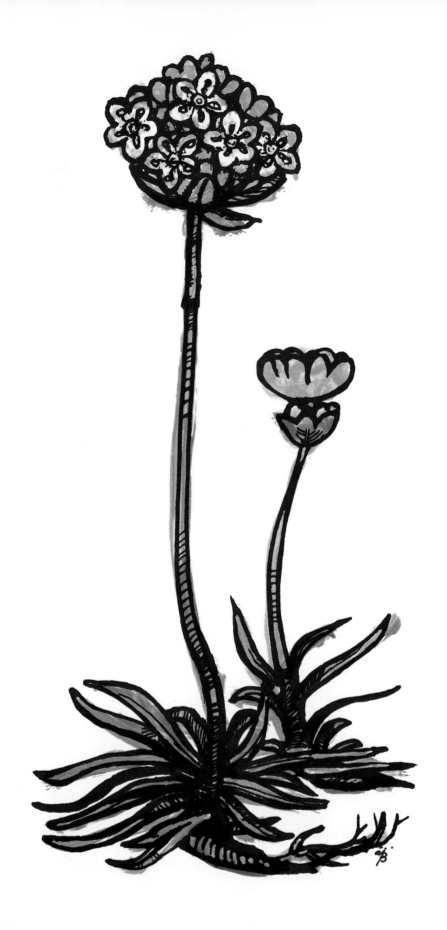

Sea-Pink

Armeria maritima
Our Lady's Cushion
(P)

∽ Meditation ∾

To be inventive with the simple things—seeds, silk, pods and tendrils—what wealth, what contentment! This is thrift. To thrift belongs prudence, planning, preparation. To thrift belongs the careful management of resources. Thrift indeed becomes a cushion for the times to come.

Scripture tells us, Mary, that you traveled from your home in Nazareth to your cousin Elizabeth in the hill country, to Bethlehem, to Egypt, to Cana, in concern for your son to the Sea of Galilee, and to Jerusalem on more than one occasion. Were you creative then and satisfied with the simple things? Teach me to see the beauty of simple things.

❧ Legend ❧

The blossoms of this plant, shaped like miniature cushions, formed a place for Mary to sit on the flight into Egypt. The journey was long, and Mary would have been tired, traveling by donkey with her infant while her husband, Joseph, walked alongside. When they stopped, Mary would have looked for a place to rest and nurse her child.

Leaving the garden at Matariyeh, the Holy Family made their way to the fortified Roman town of Babylon, now known as Old Cairo. The grotto where the travelers rested is said to be under one of the old churches in the area. In 1244 an old bishop of Acre, returning from the Crusades, reported seeing at Cairo an ancient date tree, which had spontaneously bent its branches toward Mary so she could eat its fruit. Jesus had blessed the tree and said it would be one of the trees in paradise; he called it the palm of victory. *Cairo* means "victory" in Greek.

Hazel, witch elm and the weeping willow were also said to have given shade while the family rested. Another legend tells of the palm tree, which bowed its branches to shade the Holy Family at Jesus' command. The Holy Child is seen stretching out his hand toward a branch in a painting by Antonello Mellone. In the "Flight into Egypt," a painting by Gaudenzia Ferarri, a palm-tree in the background slants its branches toward the Holy Family.

Tradition says that the Blessed Mother earned her living by weaving linen and Joseph worked as carpenter and builder during the seven years that they were in Egypt. It is told that an angel offered blossoms of thrift to Mary as a pincushion. One writer suggests that this legend comes from one of the sketches of Our Lady's flowers issued by the Medici Society in London in the nineteenth century. Another legend says that Mary used the blossoms of thrift as a cushion for her hard stool at her home in Nazareth.

The flower was considered a symbol of the Virgin Mary and it is thought that the serrated edges of the flower petals represented tongues of flame of the Holy Spirit descending on Mary at Pentecost. It blooms during May, at Pentecost time.

Sea-pink, or thrift, a dwarf evergreen which thrives when showered with salt-spray from the sea, was known as Our Lady's Cushion from early times. Gerard's *Herbal*, based on earlier herbals and published in 1597, speaks of "Thrift, or our Ladies Cushion." Gerard distinguishes between a kind of *Gillofloure* found in the salt marshes of England and the thrift found in the mountains near the Levant or Mediterranean Sea, the latter being larger in size. The plant is native to Europe, West Asia, North Africa and North America and grows in Iceland.

In Somerset, England, thrift was called cushings, a local version of cushions, while in Sussex thrift became swift. The blossoms were usually pink, but sometimes rose-red, lilac or white. The plant was used to edge gardens during the Middle Ages and in the sixteenth century used in knot gardens because it grew thick and bushy.

In England and Germany the name Our Lady's Cushion was also given to the low-growing, compact plants of the saxifrage family, called "rockfoil."

Armeria was the Roman name for the genus *Dianthus* (pinks); the species came to be known as sea pinks (*maritima*) because of its sea-side origin. The source of the folk name thrift is not known, but the flower was at one time found on threepenny pieces in England, possibly suggesting thriftiness.

Thrift grows in Mary Gardens at Woods Hole; Portage, Michigan; Cincinnati and Knock, Ireland. It is found in the Bonnefont Cloister herb garden at The Cloisters.

"Many women have done excellently, but you surpass them all. Charm is deceitful, and beauty is vain, but a woman who fears the Lord is to be praised. Give her a share in the fruit of her hands, and let her works praise her in the city gates."

— PROVERBS 31:29-31

Forget-me-not

Myosotis scorpioides
Eyes of Mary

(B)

∞ Meditation ∞

The ancients called our eyes the windows of the soul. Words are not needed when our eyes speak. Others know we wish them well by the way we look at them. The blue and gold forget-me-nots ask us to view all we see as Mary would, through eyes reflecting paradise-bright, clear and kind.

Mary, when you looked at your Child-God you could not help but reflect him. To look at you is to see him. To look at you reminds us of the paradise he came to restore. Forget-me-nots remind us of that paradise. Help us to keep our eyes fixed on him as you did.

∞ Legend ∞

The young Jesus, looking into his mother's eyes one day in front of their home in Nazareth said: "Mother, your eyes are so beautiful, everyone looks at them in wonder. What a pity those who will be born in future generations will not be able to behold them. Because in your eyes one can see my paradise, and whoever looks into them cannot help but be drawn toward it." Then he touched her eyelids and passed his hands over the ground as though sowing seeds. Immediately forget-me-nots sprang up, hundreds of tiny blue eyes with golden centers, as a reminder for people of future generations of Our Lady's pure eyes.

Forget-me-nots are among the many flowers and herbs that remind us of Mary.

In May, 1858, Louis Gemminger, then pastor of St. Peter's Church in Munich, Germany, delivered a series of reflections in honor of the Blessed Virgin Mary in nearby Ingolstadt. On each day in Mary's month, he reflected on a different flower, weaving a wreath of flowers for her. On the last day, he spoke of the forget-me-not, which "speaks to us of the heavenly forget-me-not, Mary, whom the Church salutes with the title, 'Virgo Amabilis,' 'Virgin most Amiable'.... The flower grows very abundantly, and reminds us of the many graces which we receive through Mary." The pastor ended with a poem:

> Accept the wreath your children wove,
> 'Twas made with grateful, trusting love;
> And while we lay it at your feet,
> "Forget-me-not" the flowers repeat.

During the nineteenth century Mary became the *Mater Amabilis*. She was no longer enthroned on clouds or held in mid-air by angels. The Virgin Mother now was depicted as dwelling on earth, in half-length paintings of the Madonna holding her Child in her arms. These smaller works were intended for oratories, private or wayside chapels, and for the studies, libraries and chambers of the devout, in contrast to larger and grander depictions of Mary found in churches and cathedrals. Some of the oldest pictures of the *Mater Amabilis* were the ancient portraits of the Madonna, popularly attributed to Saint Luke.

Other versions of the *Mater Amabilis* pictured the Virgin and Child seated in a landscape, often within the mystical enclosed garden—the *hortus conclusus* of the Song of Solomon: "A garden locked is my sister, my bride." In the "Madonna" by Albrecht Durer a loose fence of stakes encloses her, and in the Madonna attributed to Filippino Lippi a balustrade forms the mystical garden.

Called *Les Yeux de Notre Dame* (the Eyes of Our Lady), the forget-me-not has been the symbol of remembrance of France since at least the fourteenth century. In Italy it is called *non ti scordar di me* (do not forget me).

A legend tells of God walking through the Garden of Eden after the creation. Noticing the small blue flower, he asks its name. Overcome by shyness, the flower whispers, "I'm afraid I've forgotten, Lord." God answers, "Forget-me-not. And I will not forget thee." A different version has Adam forgetting to name the flower. When it asked for a name, Adam said, "You shall be forget-me-not."

The flower was found in medieval Paradise Gardens and appears in paintings as early as the fifteenth century. The Virgin holds a forget-me-not in her hands in the fifteenth-century "Madonna and Child," by a member of the Milanese school. The flower is found with roses and tulips in a study of flowers by Jan Brueghel (1568-1625).

Forget-me-nots are found in the Cuxa Cloister garth garden, in the enclosed courtyard of a typical medieval monastery, at The Cloisters. They grow in Mary Gardens in Annapolis, Cincinnati, Portage, Woods Hole and Knock.

"Blessed are the eyes that see what you see!"

— LUKE 10:23

Yellow Lady Slipper

Cypripedium calceolus
Our Lady's Slipper

(P)

∽ Meditation ∾

Slippers, sandals, shoes... Scripture says: "How beautiful upon the mountains are the feet of the messenger who announces peace, who brings good news, who announces salvation, who says to Zion, 'Your God reigns.'"

Mary, these happy, holy words are from the generations that had gone before you. Were you aware of them, and did you remember them when your little son decked your toes with beautiful, bright flowers? Did you in turn play the games we love to play with the toes of little children, as you all the while repeated the songs of your people? Was not your child the one who was to come, the one who would announce peace and salvation? He was to be called holy, the Son of the Most High. This you had heard; this much you knew. But all the rest?

The rest became for you an incredible, mysterious journey of faith. You who walked before him, and with him, now learned to follow him. Teach us, Mary, to be ever with him, as you were.

∽ Legend ∽

As a little boy, Jesus thrust his mother's foot into the tiny opening of the flower. It is told that in medieval times children liked to think of Jesus, as a baby boy, easing his mother's foot into the fairy slipper.

The boy Jesus grew up in Nazareth, where the Holy Family settled on their return to Galilee after Herod's death. They went to their hometown, where they lived for thirty years, after Joseph received a warning not to go to Bethlehem.

Nazareth was an obscure little town, surrounded on all sides by rugged hills. It was looked down on by Jews as incapable of producing anything good. Here the Holy Family lived in a humble home, probably two rooms built of small stones covered with clay which was sun-dried and then white-washed. A small yard at the side of the house was Joseph's workshop, and here Jesus spent his days, learning his father's craft.

Climbing one of the hills, Jesus could see the mountains of Galilee to the north, Mount Tabor and the Sea of Galilee to the east, and Little Hermon and the Mountain of Samaria towering in the south. Looking west he saw the blue outlines of Mount Carmel and the Mediterranean Sea.

Herbs and wildflowers grew in the fields and hills surrounding the town. When Jesus walked there with his mother, he saw snowdrops, violets, pinks and anemones, which grew in profusion. He saw rosemary, juniper, mint and rue. These flowers of the fields he called the "lilies of the field."

Lotus corniculatus (bird's-foot trefoil), also known as Lady's Slipper, is said to have blossomed wherever Our Lady and her little son walked. In France it was called *Le Pied de Bon Dieu*, the Feet of Our Lord.

A nineteenth-century writer of flower lore noted that:

> Many of the names by which our commonest flowers are known are not confined to England, but crop up in Germany and Scandinavia in but slightly altered forms. Thus every boy and girl delights in plucking the pretty little flower (*Lotus corniculatus*) which grows in the meadows, and is known as Lady's Slipper, Shoes and Stockings...or Boots and Shoes. In Germany, this flower is sometimes....called Mary's Shoe (*Marien-Schuh*) and Mary's Slipper (*Marien Pantoffel*).

In the sixteenth century, Rembert Dodoens called *Cypripedium calceolus*, known as the yellow Lady's Slipper of Eurasia, *Marienshoen*, or Mary's Shoe. In old Dutch it was called *Cypripedium calceolus Mariae*. Gerard, English herbalist of the same era, said Our Lady's Slipper grew in the mountains of Germany, Hungary and Poland, adding that he had acquired a specimen, which grew in his garden. The illustration in his *Herbal* is titled *Calceolus Maria. Calceolus* means "small shoe" or "half-boot" in Latin.

Cypripedium is the botanical name for a genus of hardy orchids, commonly known as lady slippers, and native to Eurasia and North America. *Lotus corniculatus* is native to Europe and refers to a later species of lily now known as lady fingers or birds-foot trefoil but earlier known as lady slipper. The orchid genus *Paphiopedilum*, native to tropical Asia, is perhaps most widely known as lady slipper today.

The Yellow Lady Slipper is found in the Garden of Our Lady at Woods Hole.

"My steps have held fast in your paths; my feet have not slipped."

— PSALMS 17:5

Fuchsia

Fuchsia magellanica and *F. hybrida*
Our Lady's Eardrop

(A)

∽ Meditation ∽

A baby's fascinated play—tugging at his mother's ear, exploring ears, mouth, nose, the softness of her skin—brings a smile to those who watch. Lovers, even little ones like this child, deck the beloved with lovely things, tuck flowers in her hair, make wreaths to bring her joy.

Mary, if such is the love between anyone who loves and the one who receives, how much more must have been the love the Christ Child bestowed on you when he clothed you with his light and made you ready to journey with him in faith! My Mary Garden reminds me of this covenanted love, this exchange of hearts, of interests and all that belongs to both. When I look at my garden, let me remember first the child who grew to manhood in your home.

The gently drooping flowers with white outer leaves and cerise, purple or pink petals resemble eardrops or pendant earrings, and it is said that Jesus may have playfully hung flower jewels of ruby and amethyst colors on his mother's ears.

In Devonshire, England, the old folks said Our Lady's Eardrop was the only name they had ever known for the flower. Chroniclers write that their forefathers, on first seeing the flowers and noticing how they resembled eardrops, named them in Mary's honor.

Because of her devotion to Mary, England has been known as Mary's Dowry since the fourteenth century when Edward III is said to have offered England to Our Lady as her dowry. In 1399 Thomas Arundel, archbishop of Canterbury, wrote:

> The contemplation of the great mystery of the Incarnation has drawn all Christian nations to venerate her from whom come the first beginnings of our redemption. But we English, being the servants of her special inheritance and her own Dowry, as we are commonly called, ought to surpass others in the fervor of our praises and devotion.

The designation disappeared during the Reformation of the sixteenth century, but England was reconsecrated to Mary in the nineteenth century, by Cardinal Wiseman in 1867 and Cardinal Vaughan in 1893.

Mary was so much a part of the life of the faithful that she was continually honored in legend and with flowers that reflected her purity, glory and sorrow. It may be that pious persons named the blossoms Our Lady's Eardrops as their way of paying tribute to Mary, who through her ears "heard the word of God, and kept it."

The tradition of adorning Mary with flowers comes from the early centuries of Christianity. Flowers were placed on her altars and her statues were decorated with flowers on her feast days. During the Middle Ages May became Mary's month and she was again honored with flowers. In the United States the custom developed of placing a wreath of flowers on Mary's statue on the first day of May.

Symbolism was used to help the faithful, especially those who could not read, understand the teachings of the Church. The purple blooms of the fuchsia were said to recall the Passion of Jesus, as Mary might have looked back on it in later years, after the Resurrection and Ascension of Jesus.

The fuchsia plant is native to Mexico, South America and New Zealand.

There are two stories of how it came to be cultivated in England—one that in 1788 a Captain Firth brought a plant to Kew Gardens, London, and nursery-man James Lee propagated it; the other, that Lee found the plant growing in the window of a house in Wapping, Essex, and purchased it from the wife (in another version the widowed mother) of the sailor who had brought it home from the mountains of Chile.

In Chile and Argentina the *magellanica* variety grows to twelve feet or more, while the hybrid variety grows to six feet in Mexico. The plant grows in gardens in the southern United States, but in cooler climates is grown in greenhouses for pots and hanging baskets.

Touch-me-not (*Impatiens biflora*) is also known as Lady's Eardrop. Balsam (*Impatiens capensis*) is known as Our Lady's Earrings.

> *"Awake, O north wind,*
> *and come, O south wind!*
> *Blow upon my garden*
> *that its fragrance may be wafted abroad.*
> *Let my beloved come to his garden,*
> *and eat its choicest fruits…*
> *My beloved has gone down to his garden,*
> *to the beds of spices,*
> *to pasture his flock in the gardens,*
> *and to gather lilies."*
>
> — SONG OF SOLOMON 4:16, 6:2

Strawberry

Fragaria vesca
Fruitfulness of Mary

(P)

❧ Meditation ❧

Sometimes medieval artists painted Mary in a robe woven with strawberry patterns. The strawberry is a fruit that has no stone, no thorns and can be eaten whole. Hence it is a reminder of paradise, where the gifts were gathered in love's effortless toil. Its white blossom signified to the painter Christ's incarnation in the Spirit-filled fruitfulness of the Virgin Mary whose cooperation helps to restore the lost garden.

The strawberry pattern, symbolizing abundant fruitfulness and woven into Mary's garment, also reminds us of the gifts of the Holy Spirit. We do not keep them for ourselves; they are meant to be shared, poured out for the wholesomeness of the Church and all her children.

The lowly little strawberry sends its runners quietly along the ground looking for places to attach itself and form a new plant. In our gardens, the strawberry takes patience and work. Its runners must be carefully transplanted to ensure new growth. It is the same with the divine gifts. Mary, show us how to cultivate them and share them.

⌘ Legend ⌘

A German legend says that Our Lady would go berry-hunting with the children on June 24, Saint John the Baptist's Day. Also on that day no mother who had lost a child would taste a strawberry, for if she did her little one would get none in paradise because Mary would say to the child, "You must stand aside, for your mother has already eaten your share, and so none remains for you!"

The strawberry symbolized the fruitfulness of Mary. In the fifteenth-century painting, "The Virgin and the Strawberries" by an Upper Rhenish Master of Paradise Garden, Mary is seated on a bench of strawberry plants. Strawberry was a symbol of the Virgin Birth because of its unusual botanical characteristic of being in flower and fruit at the same time.

The white flowers of strawberry plants are depicted in another fifteenth-century painting by the same Upper Rhenish artist. Known as "Paradise Garden," the work is sometimes called a Mary Garden and is full of Christian symbolism. Mary and her child appear in the forefront, and the garden is filled with lilies of the valley, iris, white lilies and other flowers associated with Mary.

Renaissance artists depicted the Virgin Mary wearing a dress decorated with strawberries, and in southern Europe, where statues of Mary have wardrobes for each festival, the flowers often adorned her gowns. Mary's mantle is bedecked with strawberries in the "Mystic Marriage of Saint Catherine" by Lorenzo il Salimbeni da Sanseverino.

The low-growing strawberry was sometimes accompanied by the modest violet as a symbol of humility. Both are seen in the meadow where the Virgin Mary sits in Giovanni di Paolo's "Madonna of Humility" and in Botticelli's "Madonna and Child with Four Angels."

The plant became a symbol of the Incarnation of Christ because it has white flowers and blooms in the spring. It appeared in paintings of the Nativity, adoration of the Magi, Holy Family and other scenes where the Incarnation of Christ was represented. Jesus holds strawberries in his hands in the "Holy Family" by Signorelli, and strawberry plants are depicted in "Rest During the Flight" by Hans Baldung-Grien.

Gerard, the Elizabethan botanist, said that Virgil and Ovid called the berries *fraga*, for "fragrant." In French they are called *fraises*. The plant is first mentioned in a plant list in 995 when the teacher Aelfric compiled a vocabulary list that included more than two hundred herbs and trees. The English name comes from the verb "to strew," referring to the leafy runners which cover the ground.

The plant was popular in medieval kitchen and monastery gardens as well as Paradise Gardens. At The Cloisters strawberries grow in the Bonnefont Cloister herb garden, containing plants of the Middle Ages, and in the Trie Cloister, containing plants depicted in the Unicorn Tapestries.

"All these were constantly devoting themselves to prayer, together with certain women, including Mary the mother of Jesus, as well as his brothers. Divided tongues, as of fire, appeared among them, and a tongue rested on each of them. All of them were filled with the Holy Spirit."

— ACTS 1:14; 2:3-4

Cuckoo Flower

Cardamine pratensis
Meadow Cress,
Our Lady's Smock

(P)

∞ Meditation ∞

Our hands are busy with many things: giving, receiving, doing, undoing, creating, destroying, weaving patterns of life from moment to moment. Thread after thread bears mystery and memory.

Mary, you are a weaver: weaving temple linen, swaddling clothes and within your womb, the weaving of God made flesh to dwell among us. Dress us in your smock, Mary, that we may weave as you have done.

Jesus gave this flower to his mother in honor of the seamless robe of Calvary. The flowers suggest fine linens laid out to bleach: either Our Lady's garments or those made by her hands.

Mary helped support her family in Egypt by weaving linen. A passage in the apocryphal Protoevangelium of James tells us that Mary was a weaver even as a young girl. The child Mary and seven other virgins were brought together by the council of priests to weave a veil for the temple. The virgins drew lots "and the lot of the true purple and the scarlet fell unto Mary, and she took them and went unto her house.....and Mary took the scarlet and began to spin it."

The lace-makers of Brussels knew of Mary's skills with fiber arts. They would pray to Mary that their work might stay as white as snow on August 5, the *Feast of Maria ad Nives* or *Notre Dame aux Neiges* (Our Lady of the Snows), the anniversary of the dedication of the Basilica of Our Lady of the Snows (*Santa Maria Maggiore*) in Rome.

Saint Bonaventure, Franciscan theologian of the thirteenth century, tells of a tradition that when the Holy Family was in Egypt, they were so poor that Mary was forced to go door to door, begging for flax to spin into garments for her child.

From Jacob Grimm's *Teutonic Mythology* comes another reference to Mary weaving and an explanation of how even cobwebs were named after Mary:

> The white threads cover the fields at the beginning of spring,
> and still more of autumn; the spring tissue is also called
> maidensummer, Mary's yarn, Mary's thread...The flying gos-
> samer (cobwebs) in autumn is in vulgar opinion the thread
> spun by elves and dwarfs; the Christians named it
> Marienfaden (-thread), Mariensommer, because Mary too was
> imagined spinning and weaving.

Mary probably learned other domestic arts. In a painting of "The Girlhood of Mary Virgin" by Dante Gabriel Rossetti, she is seated at an embroidery frame and works on a piece of red material. Her mother, Saint Anne, is at her side.

The flowers of meadow cress are known as Our Lady's Smock in Cheshire, England, because the flowers look like little smocks. When they cover a meadow the flowers give the appearance of little smocks laid out to dry. They are known as *La Chemise de Notre Dame* and similar names in many parts of Europe.

Our Lady's Smock became known as ladysmocks after the Protestant Reformation, when devotion to Mary was suppressed and the prefix "our" was dropped from many plant names, such as Our Lady's Slipper and Our Lady's Candlestick. The name "Lady" in plants is almost always a post-Reformation contraction of "Our Lady."

In the sixteenth century the plant grew wild in Italy and England. Shakespeare speaks of "lady-smocks all silver-white" being "hung out to dry." The moisture-loving herb grows in northern North America, Europe and Asia.

Other plants also known as Lady's Smock are marsh marigold (*Caltha palustris*) and in Norfolk, England, Canterbury bells (*Campanula medium*).

*"Whatever your hand finds to do,
do with your might...."*

— ECCLESIASTES 9:10

Harebell

Campanula rotundifolia
Bluebell
Our Lady's Thimble
(P)

✤ Meditation ✤

Stitch after stitch, seed after seed, seconds move forward in the sacred space called time. We plant, we reap, we weave, we sew. We name these things in the rhythms of life. Bead after bead moves through our fingers as we contemplate Incarnation and its completion on Calvary followed by Easter morning.

Mary, the thimble shields from needle prick, but no shield held back the blows or the dice used to gamble for his garments. When the pricks, the blows, the risks heap pain on every side, give us calm to remember, our sister, how you stood at his side, even then.

The bell-shaped flowers, resembling tiny thimbles, were named after Our Lady to honor her working hands as she made Jesus' clothes, including the seamless robe he was wearing before he was crucified.

The story of the naming of the flower is told in the following lines from a longer poem titled "Our Lady's Thimble":

> Our Lady sat by her Mother's side,
> And sewed her seam with a housewife's pride.
> Mary, the child of Anne.

Mary pricks her finger and her mother tells her to rest, then covers the wounded finger with a healing salve and a cloth bandage.

> But the maiden smiled as she softly bent
> And gathered a flower at her side that leant,
> A flower with cups of blue.

> See, this small cup will my finger shield,
> And be known henceforward in hedge or field
> As the Thimble and shield of Mary.

As a young girl Mary went to the temple, where she learned to spin wool, weave linens and embroider the tapestries that hung there. At home she sewed, instructed by her mother.

Mary's many homemaking skills are described in a book published in 1900, which describes "a set of twelve prints, executed in the Netherlands, exhibiting a sort of history of the childhood of Christ, and his training under the eye of the mother." The book is titled *Jesu Christi dei Domini Salvatoris nostri Infantia*, "The Infancy of our Lord God and Saviour Jesus Christ," and the "title-page is surrounded by a border composed of musical instruments, spinning-wheels, distaffs, and other implements of female industry, intermixed with all kinds of masons' and carpenters' tools."

The book describes the drawings, in which Mary is shown engaged in various needle-craft and weaving activities. She does needlework while Jesus sleeps in his cradle, measures linen while Saint Anne looks on and Jesus blows soap-bubbles, knits a stocking while Jesus helps Joseph build a boat. She is shown seated at her spinning-wheel, carding wool or flax, winding thread, reeling off a skein of thread, and spinning with a distaff.

Joseph is shown erecting a fence around a garden in the last scene. Jesus, assisted by angels, fastens the palings together and Mary weaves a garland of roses.

Bluebells are said to grow near Saint Dominic's thirteenth-century resting place in Bologna, Italy, and to be associated with the rosary, which he dedicated to Our Lady.

In the early sixteenth century the flowers grew in St. Mary's garden at Melrose Abbey in Scotland. The abbey was founded in 1136 by David I and dedicated to the Virgin Mary. In Scotland the flowers were known as the bluebells of Scotland and were identified with the cross of Jesus. An old verse tells that:

> The blue Harebells the fields adorn
> Against the day of Holie Cross.

The graceful flowers grew wild on the moors, hills and roadsides of England and were said to be found in gardens of Shakespearean times. They grow in the Mary Garden at Woods Hole and in the Bonnefont Cloister herb garden at The Cloisters, where they are called Canterbury bells.

Foxglove (*Digitalis purpurea*) and germander speedwell (*Veronica chamaedrys*) are also known as Lady's Thimble.

*"For thus said the Lord God,
the Holy One of Israel,
'In returning and rest
you shall be saved;
in quietness and in trust
shall be your strength.'"*

— ISAIAH 30:15

Lavender

Lavandula officinalis
Mary's Drying Plant

(P)

❧ Meditation ❧

Lavender, a million tiny blue blossoms gathered to sachets to sweeten, freshen, charm. A million seeds floating hidden in the wind, bear flower and fruit. A million faces neon-lit and rushing everywhere, eluding our ability to touch their hearts and make a difference anywhere.

Mary, stop by our garden for a while, look at our lavender, ponder and share its treasures. What would your son tell us? How can the gardens of our hearts become better places to be?

∞ Legend ∞

After Mary had washed Jesus' clothes and was looking for a place to hang them to dry, she saw a gray bush of lavender and on its branches she spread the snow-white baby clothes. The sun and the wind dried the clothes and when Mary came to gather them, the clothes smelled sweet and clean and the bushes were fragrant with the sweet scent that lavender now has. It is said that the fragrance which came from the earthly body of the son of God was transferred to the plant, giving it its unique scent. The same story is told of rosemary and other sweet-scented shrubs.

Lavender was said to be one of the plants most loved by the Blessed Virgin because it represented purity, cleanliness and virtue. It was considered sacred to Mary because of its association with spotlessness and chastity.

Not much is known about the period of Mary's life when Jesus was a child. One writer notes that "Not even legend has cast a light upon [these] years of Our Lady's life. [Jesus] dwelt with her, and that was enough." Imaginative artists, however, created domestic scenes of Mary's life and her family.

About the middle of the fifteenth century artists had begun to paint domestic groups of our Blessed Mother and her child, surrounded by Joseph, Elizabeth and her son, and others. Pietro Perugino painted a large family group of Mary holding her child, with her mother Anne resting her hands on Mary's shoulders, and a group of boys and women representing cousins and other relatives of Our Lady.

A painting of the Holy Family by Schongauer in the latter part of the fifteenth century shows Mary seated in her home, plucking at a bunch of grapes in her hand. She holds the infant Jesus in one arm and Joseph looks on. In "The Home at Nazareth," an engraving by Albrecht Durer of about the same period, Joseph is shown working at carpentry, Mary holds a skein of wool in her hands, Jesus sleeps in a cradle and angels hover over all.

Lavender is not depicted in these paintings, but it was grown in monastic kitchen and infirmary gardens of the Middle Ages. Hildegard of Bingen listed it in 1150 as one of the garden herbs known to her. Lavender was grown for edging in knot gardens, in hedges of Italian gardens and for scent in French gardens.

In medieval times, lavender was considered a most versatile flower. It was used for scenting and freshening linens. Bed sheets and shirts thrown over a full-grown lavender plant to bleach in the sun took on the sweet scent as did linens stored with the flower heads. Pots of lavender stood in front of windows to sweeten rooms in summer; in the winter months bunches of dried lavender stems were hung in cupboards and on walls for the same purpose.

Lavender was one of the major herbs used for strewing in homes and public places. Together with rosemary, woodruff and balm, it was scattered on church and theater floors for health reasons, to ward off fevers and dispel odors. People carried small bunches of flowers and herbs, called "tussie mussies," for their scent.

During the seventeenth century, it is said, lawyers and judges carried small bunches of herbs to protect them from the plague and other diseases. Lavender, rosemary and rue were scattered on courtroom floors. Early in the eighteenth century the recorder of the city of London carried a "posy," a small bouquet of seven herbs: chamomile, hyssop, lavender, lemon balm, marjoram, rue and sage, as protection from infectious diseases. Church pews were still strewn with those herbs in the nineteenth century.

The name comes from the Latin word lavare "to wash" because of the ancient Roman custom of using the leaves and flowers to scent the bath water. The plant was grown by Arab botanists in eleventh-century Spain. It was native to France and western Mediterranean countries and was probably introduced to Britain by the Romans.

Early Lavender was called "stickadove" and Gerard, the sixteenth-century English herbalist, called it "Lavander Spike," because the "floures grow at the top of the branches, spike fashion, of a blew colour."

Lavender grows in the Mary Garden in Annapolis and in Knock, Ireland. It is found in the Bonnefont Cloister herb garden of The Cloisters.

"Abide in me as I abide in you.
Just as the branch cannot bear fruit
by itself unless it abides in the vine,
neither can you unless you abide in me....
As the Father has loved me, so I have loved
you: abide in my love.... I have said these
things to you so that my joy may be in you,
and that your joy may be complete."

— JOHN 15:4, 9, 11

Marigold

Calendula officinalis
Scottish or pot marigold
Mary's Gold

(A)

☙ Meditation ☙

Pick golden blossoms one by one. Weave garlands of gold and lay them at her feet. She is the dwelling place of God, the golden tabernacle where once he lay. Our gathered flowers adorn her, the living temple of the Lord. His Spirit remains her fullness forever. She will not keep the garlands for herself. These golden gifts will pass through her hands, given to the King of kings, her Child and God.

The marigold garlands will fade. Nonetheless, for the splendor of their moment they signify a more precious gold that will not whither. It is the gold of the word of God, tested by fire, proven true in the crucible of life.

Mary, you heard the word of God and became ark of his indwelling. His words did not dry up and shrivel in your heart. They remained fresh, fragrant, strong, powerfully transforming your life day by day. The gold of Christ's word and wisdom was your richness. Give us your gold, Mary, give us your wealth.

⊗ Legend ⊗

Tradition says that Our Lady used the golden blossoms as coins and that her garments were adorned with the flowers. Early Christians placed *calendula* around statues of Mary, offering the blossoms in place of coins, and called them Mary's Gold. It is told that during the flight into Egypt the Holy Family encountered robbers. When they snatched the family purse from Mary, out came Mary's Gold.

During the Middle Ages the plant was grown in monastery and convent gardens. It was dedicated to the Virgin Mary and called marygold or marybud because it bloomed during all of the feast days of the Virgin Mary. The flowers were often made into garlands and used for decorating churches on her feast days, especially the Feast of the Annunciation, March 25.

The marigold is connected with the Virgin Mary under its Latin name, *caltha*, in a fourteenth-century hymn in her honor. Gualterus Wiburnus wrote:

> *Ave thymum, caltha, rosa...*   Hail thyme, marigold, rose...

It is said to represent the golden rays of glory that are often depicted around the head of the Blessed Virgin.

Marigolds were known to the ancient Romans. Fire-colored marigolds are mentioned in a gardening poem by Columella, who wrote during the reign of Augustus in Rome. They appear in a fourth-century book on agriculture, *De Re Rustica*, by Palladius, and many subsequent lists of plants and flowers.

Palladius's book, written in poetic style, is remembered for its evocation of spring and its sensitivity to the beauty of plants. Marigolds and other flowers symbolic of Mary flourish in this excerpt from "Book X":

> Now when the earth, its clear divisions marked
> > as with a comb, shining, from squalor free,
> Shall claim her seeds, 'tis time to paint the earth
> With varied flowers, like stars brought down from heaven,
> White snow-drops and the yellow-shining eyes
> > Of marigolds and fair narcissus blooms,
> With Fierce lions' gaping mouths and the white cups
> Of Blooming lilies and the corn flag bloom,
> Snow-white or blue. Then let the violet
> > Be planted, which lies pale upon the ground
> > Or blooms with gold and purple blossoms crowned,
> Likewise the rose too full of maiden blush....

Marigolds are remembered in art and literature of the Middle Ages. Perdita, the lost princess in Shakespeare's *The Winter's Tale*, grows the flowers in her rustic garden and tells of "The marigold, that goes to bed wi' th' sun..." (Act IV, Scene iv). In Shakespeare's *Cymbeline* we find that: "...winking Mary-buds begin / To ope their golden eyes" (Act II, Scene iii).

Marigolds are among the flowers depicted on the steps of the throne in the painting, "Madonna and Child Enthroned with Saints," by Carlo Crivelli, signed and dated 1491. They are found in the Unicorn Tapestries of the late fifteenth century and in Bernardino Luini's "Madonna and Child with the Infant Saint John," painted in the sixteenth century.

The Latin name, *Calendula*, was given because it blooms in every month of the year in warm climates and was thought to bloom on the first day of the month. Marigolds were called *Lus Mairi* in Gaelic and *Marienbloem* in German.

A search of old herbals reveals that the name Marygold is applied to several other flowers: the African marigold (*Tagetes erecta*), French marigold (*Tagetes patula*), marsh marigold (*Caltha palustris*), annual chrysanthemum (*Chrysanthemum segetum*) and Livingston daisy (*Mesembryanthemum criniflorum*).

The flowers grow in the Bonnefont Cloister herb garden, representative of medieval kitchen gardens, and the Trie Cloister, containing plants and trees of the Unicorn Tapestries, in The Cloisters. They grow in Mary Gardens in Annapolis, Portage and Woods Hole and in Knock, Ireland.

*"The grass withers,
the flower fades;
but the word of our God
will stand forever."*

— ISAIAH 40:8

Lily of the Valley

Convallaria majalis
Mary's Tears
(P)

❧ Meditation ❧

The sacred text does not speak of your tears, Mary, like our legend does. It tells us instead, that you stood by the cross and you were not alone. Other women and John were also there. We wonder at the sorrow, the bitterness, the pain of this little community standing by. We know that silence alone can give voice to the moment. It is Jesus who broke the silence: "Woman, this is your son! Son, this is your mother." And John took you home.

Fragrant tiny white lily-bells tucked along a garden walk, indestructible perennial spreading roots by a shed, a thousand quiet tears bowing before the still cold winter winds, teach us of springtime and Resurrection just beyond the stone-cold tomb.

∽ Legend ∽

It was said that when Mary wept at the foot of the Cross, her tears fell to the ground and turned into the tiny fragrant blossoms of this early spring plant. In England it had the name "Our Lady's Tears" because when viewed from a distance the white flowerets gave the appearance of tear drops falling.

The lily of the valley was a symbol of the Virgin Mary because of its pure white flowers, its sweet smell and its humble appearance. It symbolized Mary's Immaculate Conception and represented the purity of body and of soul by which Mary found favor in God. Gaspare Venturini depicts lily of the valley growing near Mary's feet in "The Immaculate Conception."

In the twelfth century Adam of Saint Victor compared Mary to the lily in his poem, "*In Assumptione Beatae Virginis*":

(Maria) *flos campi, convallium*	Mary, flower of the field
Singulare lilium	Exquisite lily of the valley
Christus ex te prodiit.	Christ came forth from you.

Mary is depicted as Queen of Heaven in the 1432 altarpiece by Hubert van Eyck in the Church of Saint Bavon in Ghent. She wears a crown of gold, set with pearls, sapphires and rubies. Above the jewels are lily of the valley, roses, lilies and columbine, all flowers symbolic of Mary. Roses, flag iris and lily of the valley also appear in Jan van Eyck's "The Madonna of the Fountain" of the same period.

The lily of the valley was said to typify the meekness and "low estate" of the "handmaid of the Lord." The name indicated the "hidden" location of the flower in low places—valleys—making it another symbol of humility.

The flower was also called ladder to heaven as a symbol of the handmaid of the Lord. In the sixteenth century Joannes Ammonius Agricola called the plant Mary's Seal (*Sigillum S. Mariae*) in his *Medicinae Herbariae*.

Because it blooms around the time of the annunciation, the flower was used in Europe to decorate churches and Marian shrines on that day. It was one of several spring flowers used to decorate the altars of Lady chapels in England during May and was sometimes called the May lily. A garden devoted to growing flowers for the church was established sometime prior to the tenth century next to the Lady chapel of the original church at Winchester in England. For a long time after the chapel was destroyed, the site went by the name of Paradise.

Lily of the valley grew in the St. Mary's garden at Melrose Abbey in Scotland during the early sixteenth century. The garden contained many plants with white flowers, since white was symbolic of the Virgin's purity and holiness.

The plant was native to most European countries and has been cultivated for more than four hundred years. The genus name comes from the Latin for "valley" and is thought to refer to its original home. Its botanical name, *Convalleria majalis*, means "May lily." In Germany the flowers are called *die Maiglockenchen* or little May bells.

Lily of the valley grows in the five U. S. Mary Gardens as well as the garden in Knock, Ireland. It is called Our Lady's Tears, The Virgin's Tears and Ladder to Heaven.

"May those who sow in tears reap with shouts of joy. Those who go out weeping, bearing the seed for sowing, shall come home with shouts of joy, carrying their sheaves."

— PSALM 126:5-6

Roses and Lilies

Rosa
Red Rose, Our Lady's Rose
(P)

Lilium
White Lily, Mary's Lily
(P)

⁓ Meditation ⁓

A gardener knows the dying of the garden, but also knows its awakening. Both are necessary for the garden's fruitfulness.

Your destiny is our destiny, Mary. Your life mirrors to us what ours is to be, if we but faithfully follow Christ Jesus, who is the way, truth and life. We look forward, Mary, to our gathering in and homecoming; we look forward to meeting you. Center us as you were centered. May Jesus alone be the norm, form and goal of our lives.

∽ Legend ∾

During the second century it was told that one day about twelve years after the death of her son, Mary awakened with an inexpressible longing for him. As she wept for him an angel came to her and said, "Hail, Blessed Mary. Behold, I have brought unto thee a branch of the palm of Paradise." The angel told her that in three days she would be called forth from her body to where her son awaited her. The palm was to be carried before her bier.

Mary asked that her sons and brothers—the apostles—be gathered near her, so that she could see them before she died and so they could bury her. The angel told her the apostles would be with her that day, and they were immediately plucked up by clouds wherever they were preaching and transported to her house.

Then Jesus came to her and said: "Come, my chosen one, and I shall place thee upon my throne, for I have desired thy beauty!" Mary answered: "My heart is ready, O Lord, my heart is ready!" And her soul went forth out of her body and flew upward in the arms of her son. Jesus told the apostles to "Carry the body of the Virgin, my mother, to the valley of Josaphat, and lay it in the new tomb which ye will find there; and await me for three days, until I come to you!" As Mary rose upwards she was surrounded with red roses and white lilies.

Three days later Jesus appeared before the apostles and said, "What grace and honour, think ye, shall I now confer upon my mother?" The apostles answered, "It seems right that as thou has vanquished death, so thou, Jesus, shouldst raise up the body of thy mother and place her at thy right hand for all eternity." Jesus nodded and an angel appeared, presenting Mary's soul to him. Her soul entered her body, then Mary came forth from the tomb and was assumed into heaven, accompanied by a chorus of angels.

Thomas, however, was not present, and when he arrived refused to believe that this had happened. He asked that her tomb be opened and when it was opened it contained only lilies and roses. It is also told that Mary's girdle fell unopened into his hands, so that he might know she had been assumed. In another version, Thomas looks up and sees Mary slowly rising toward heaven and she throws her girdle down to him.

Roses and lilies have been symbols of Mary since earliest times. The rose, emblematic of her purity, glory and sorrow, represented her as Queen of Heaven and was a symbol of her love for God and for Christ, her son. The lily represented her immaculate purity, her innocence and virginity.

A hymn by Saint Peter Damian, who lived in the eleventh century, said that Mary was covered with roses, attired with the lily and exalted by all the flowers of virtue:

The vestivit lilio, sparsit in te rosam
   He clothed you with lilies, covered you with roses
Te virtutis floribus fecit speciosam
   He embellished you with the flowers of virtue

Pope Innocent III (1161-1216) wrote these lines in a hymn titled "The Assumption of the Virgin":

Da rosas, sparge lilia:	Give roses, throw lilies
Nam regina	For the queen
Nunc divina	Now divine
Haec subivit atria	Entered these hallowed halls

During the Middle Ages artists depicted Mary with lilies and roses in numerous scenes. In the "Enthroned Madonna" of Giotto, two angels offer vases filled with lilies and roses. In Fra Angelico's "Madonna and Child," the Virgin holds a vase of three roses and a stem of lilies. Roses and lilies are in the center of a painting of "The Immaculate Conception" by Francia. Mary was depicted with white lilies and red roses in the "Paradise Garden" of an Upper Rhenish artist of the fifteenth century.

Roses and lilies are depicted in Mary's tomb in paintings of the assumption by della Gatta, di Bicci, Raphael, Signorelli and others. Raphael and Sodoma painted roses and a single lily in Mary's tomb. Other artists filled her tomb only with roses.

Roses and lilies grow in the Mary Gardens in Annapolis, Woods Hole, Portage and Knock, Ireland.

"Listen to me, my faithful children, and blossom like a rose growing by a stream of water. Send out fragrance like incense, and put forth blossoms like a lily."

— SIRACH 39:13-14

Our Lady's Rose

Lychnis coronaria
Rose Campion
(P)

❧ Meditation ☙

Twenty centuries have passed since Jesus walked the highways of Israel. We talk of millennial turns and thresholds. We stand looking back, looking forward. Turning to the past, we hold fast to sacred texts, traditions and even to legends that link us to greater realities. The rosary fits all three of these categories. "Our Lady's saulter" or "psalter" recalls the one hundred fifty Psalms of the Hebrew Scriptures condensed and fulfilled in the Incarnation which began with an angel's greeting: *Ave*—hail—Mary, be greeted! So it came to be: Slowly through the millennia, a garland of roses, woven of prayer and meditation on the Word made flesh, has come to be known as the rosary in all its forms and varieties.

Mary, each line of your legends gives us something to ponder. What treasures of our Lord have we gathered today? Who, what, where are the thieves waiting to steal our treasure away? As we pass by our gardens in a hurry to meet deadlines and cross thresholds, do we pause to pray? Somewhere is a garland of roses long forgotten, needing to pass through fingers one by one. Pondering, praying, remembering: Where our hearts are, there will our treasure be.

∽ Legend ∾

In medieval times a lordsman went on a journey with much of his lord's treasured goods. He had to pass through a woods where he knew thieves would be waiting for him. As he entered the woods he remembered that he had not yet said "Our Lady's saulter," so he knelt down to pray. As he prayed the Virgin Mary came and placed a garland on his head and as he said each *Ave* she placed a rose in the garland that was "so bryghte that all the wood shone thereof." Finishing his prayers, he proceeded through the woods, unaware of the glorious crown on his head. When the thieves saw the roses they stood aside, allowing him to pass unharmed.

In another version a monk on a journey was praying his *Aves* when robbers approached. Our Lady appeared and began to pull roses from his lips, weaving them into a garland. As the garland grew longer the roses grew smaller, until they were the size of rosary beads. Mary placed them around the monk's neck and the thieves, seeing this miracle, renounced their sinful lives and later became monks.

There are reports of a group of miracles, compiled in the fifteenth century by a Dominican preacher, Johannes Herolt, called Discipulus, known as the Rosary series, in which the Virgin Mary saved ignorant or immoral clerks and monks from eternal damnation. The *Aves* they said to Mary in life turned to roses on their lips in death. In one legend, roses spring from the lips of a clerk who lived a disreputable life and died unrepentant but had never forgotten to kneel and weep before the Virgin's image. She appears before the clergy, who have buried him outside the cemetery, and threatens them with dread penalties if they do not dig him up and bury him in the best spot in the cemetery.

The rose campion is called *Candelaria* in Spain and Portugal, and in other parts of Europe it is Mary's Rose. The white campion (*Silene alba*) is known as *La Chandelle de Notre Dame* in France, a reminder of Candlemas Day. *Lychnis Coeli-rosa* is called rose of heaven.

Ghirlandaio added the wild white campion to the lilies and roses at the foot of the throne in the "Enthroned Madonna." The star-like form of the flower brings to mind Mary's title *Stella Maris* (Star of the Sea) as well as the starry crown described by Saint John. Rose campion is among the flowers depicted in "Paradise Garden" by the Upper Rhenish master.

Roses were cultivated in Bible times for their scent and beauty and several species, including *Rosa canina* and *Rosa phoenicia*, are native to Israel. The rose of the Bible, however, is said to refer to several different flowers. The word rose comes from a Hebrew word whose root means "bulb-like." The rose in Isaiah: "the desert shall bloom like a rose," was probably narcissus or a red tulip. The rose in the Song of Solomon, "I am a rose of Sharon," is thought to be the mountain tulip or the lily or possibly *Narcissus tazetta*. The Rose of Jericho is *Anastatica hierochuntica*.

The campion is a member of the pink family, with white, flesh-colored or purple petals. The name *lychnis* comes from the Greek for "lamp," referring to the flame-colored flowers of some species of this genus. The name *Campion* comes from *campi* in Latin and refers to its habit of growing in fields.

Rose campion grows in the Mary Garden in Portage where it is called Mary's Rose. It is found in the herb garden of the Bonnefont Cloister at The Cloisters.

"I tell you, do not be worried about your life, what you will eat, or about your body, what you will wear. Instead, strive for his kingdom, and these things will be given to you as well. Do not be afraid...Sell your possessions, and give alms. Let your treasure be things of heaven. For where your treasure is, there your heart will be, also."

— LUKE 12: 22, 31-34

Fleur-de-Lis

Iris pseudocorus
Yellow Flag Iris
(P)

☙ Meditation ❧

It is not tiring to hear a beloved person repeat our name a thousand times. Nor if someone should say, "I love you!" over and over again.

Mary, more countless than the drops in an ocean or stars in the firmament are the repetitions down the ages of those gracious words: Hail, full of grace, the Lord is with thee. We add our voices, our prayers, our roses and lilies to the wellspring of praise. If only the Holy Spirit would lend power to our lives and transform us into Christ-bearers for the world! Then we, too, could acclaim: The Lord is truly among us. Rejoice.

⊙ Legend ⊙

During the fourteenth century in France there was a wealthy knight, Salaun, who had renounced the world and entered the Cistercian Order. The former soldier was very devout but not very well educated. He could never remember more than the first two words of the *Ave Maria*, the Latin prayer to Mary, even though a teacher gave him lessons. He kept repeating the two words, "*Ave Maria, Ave Maria*," as he prayed to the Virgin. He prayed to her day and night, using only those two words. He grew old and when he died was buried in the chapel-yard of a monastery. As proof that Mary had heard his short but earnest prayer a fleur-de-lis plant sprang up on his grave, and on every flower shone in golden letters the words "*Ave Maria*." The monks, who had ridiculed him because of what they viewed as his ignorant piety, were so amazed at this sight that they cleared the earth and opened his grave. There they found the root of the plant resting on the lips of the knight. Finally, they understood his great devotion.

From ancient times the yellow iris has been considered sacred to the Virgin Mary and was one of the plants used to decorate churches on special days. In the sixth century, Gregory of Tours told the story of the priest Secerus who gathered *flores liliorum* to decorate the walls of his church.

In Chartres Cathedral in France, the famous thirteenth-century rose window of the north transept, which depicts the glorification of the Virgin, includes the fleur-de-lis, said to be a symbol of the annunciation.

In early times, both irises and daffodils were referred to as lilies. The fleur-de-lis (lily flower) is known as the lily of France and has been associated with France since the fifth century when Clovis I, king of the Franks, adopted the iris as his emblem after it saved him from defeat by the Goths. Finding himself trapped between the opposing army on one side and the Rhine River on the other, Clovis prayed to the Christian God, vowing to convert to Christianity if he could be saved. (His queen, Clothilda, a devout Christian, had been begging him since their marriage to convert to Christianity.) As he finished his prayer he noticed yellow iris growing far out into the river, indicating shallow water. Clovis took this as a sign from God and marched his troops across the river to safety. Keeping his promise, he and three thousand of his followers became Christians on Christmas Day that year.

In the twelfth century Louis VII of France used the fleur-de-lis as the emblem on his shield during the Crusades, and in the fourteenth century Charles IV included the iris on the French banner. The flower may originally have been called *fleur de Louis*, then changed to *fleur de luce* and finally *fleur-de-lis* (or Lys). The Lys is a river in France and the flowers were said to grow in profusion on its banks.

From John Gerard's *Herbal* we learn that "The water Floure de-luce or yellow Flag prospereth well in moist medowes and in the borders and brinks of Rivers, ponds and standing lakes."

Yellow flag iris (*Iris pseudacorus*) grows in the Bonnefont Cloister garden and flag iris or fleur-de-lis (*Iris germanica*) grows in the Bonnefont and Trie Cloister gardens of The Cloisters.

Several varieties of blue flag iris, including those known as Moonlight Madonna and Mary's Sword, grow in the Annapolis Mary Garden.

"Greetings, favored one!
The Lord is with you!
The Holy Spirit will come upon you,
and the power of the Most High will
overshadow you; therefore the
child to be born will be holy;
he will be called Son of God."

— LUKE 1:28, 35

Scotch Rose

Rosa spinosissima
Our Lady's Rose

(P)

∽ Meditation ∽

Commitment means choice; choice includes options. Once a choice is made, the options are settled—or should be—we think. We cannot anticipate them all, much like we cannot anticipate every weed in a garden, nor every fruit. The best we can do is delight in the adventure around the next bend and watch for the guiding hand of God to pluck the roses.

Joseph, when you took Mary and her child under your protection, did you imagine it would lead you far away from the familiar sights and sounds of your home to a foreign country? As skilled craftsman were you able to provide? Scripture calls you a man of honor, a just man. You made a commitment and you carried it out, no matter what the cost. Joseph, assist us with our gardens, with our living and our dying.

✑ Legend ✑

In Glastonbury, England, it is told that Joseph of Arimathea, a rich man who provided the tomb for Jesus' burial, raised the first Christian temple to the Blessed Virgin. The temple was destroyed during the Reformation, but a rose still grows on the spot, blooming all winter and at Christmastime.

At Hildesheim, in Germany, in the garden of the ancient abbey there, a wild rose tree said to be more than a thousand years old still grows and blossoms. Its roots are within the crypt, and tradition says that it was growing before Charlemagne laid the foundations of the cathedral. When the cathedral was burned and totally destroyed during World War II, the people of Hildesheim were devastated. The following spring, it is told, the base of the rose plant again sprouted, and the people's hope was renewed.

In the fourth century Saints Basil and Ambrose declared the rose the most perfect of flowers, saying it had been without thorns when it grew in Paradise and only developed its sharp spikes after the disobedience of Adam and Eve. Mary was called "a rose without thorns" because she was the only human person born free of original sin. An English hymn from about 1300 calls Mary a rose without thorn:

> Lavedy [Lady], flower of all thing
> *Rosa sine spina*   [Rose without thorn]
> Thu bere Jhesu, hevene king
> *Gratia devina*   [Divine grace]

During the sixth century, when the Church instituted the cult of the Virgin, the rose became the flower of the tribe of David, from which Mary and her son descended.

Beginning in the seventh century, Mary was called *Rosa Mystica*, the Mystical Rose, in recognition of the mysterious generation of Christ from her womb. Seven hundred years later Dante described Mary as the mystic rose in his *Divine Comedy*.

The glorious rose windows of the great thirteenth-century Gothic cathedrals of Europe embody the mystic rose, symbol of all creation. Most notable are the rose windows in cathedrals in France, many of them named Notre Dame. Chartres Cathedral, called the *"Rose de France,"* was entirely dedicated to the Virgin Mary. Rose windows in Reims Cathedral portray the litany of the Virgin Mary and her death. Mary is depicted with the Christ Child on her knee in the center of the west rose window of Notre Dame Cathedral in Paris and the east rose window of Laon Cathedral. In the north rose window at Notre Dame, Old Testament figures surround the Virgin Mary, who again has Christ on her knee.

In Italy, May is the Madonna's month of the rose and Mary's altars are always decorated with roses. A legend relates that the archangel Gabriel wound one hundred fifty roses into three wreaths for Mary—red roses for her sorrows, white for her joys and gold for her glory.

It is said that Saint Dominic named the rosary after this emblem of the Virgin Mary. Although there is no historical evidence to support the legend, Saint Dominic is credited with inventing the rosary. It is said that in 1214 the Virgin Mary appeared to Dominic, who was discouraged about his failure to convert the Cathars to orthodox Christianity. She was accompanied by three queens and fifty maidens, the same numbers as in the psalter, and told him, "If you would preach successfully, preach my psalter." It is said that Dominic went forth with the rosary given him by Our Lady and reconverted the Cathars to Catholicism.

Rosa spinosissima is called "Her Flower" in the Mary Garden at Woods Hole where all the roses are called "Her Flower."

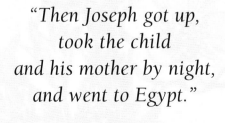

*"Then Joseph got up,
took the child
and his mother by night,
and went to Egypt."*

— MATTHEW 2:14

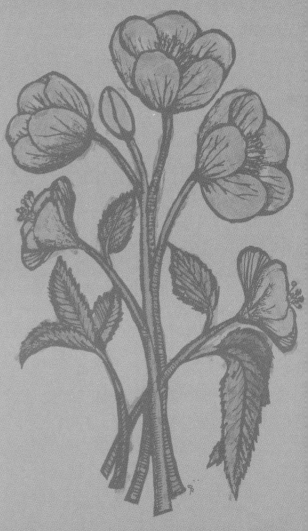

PART THREE

MARY
GARDENS

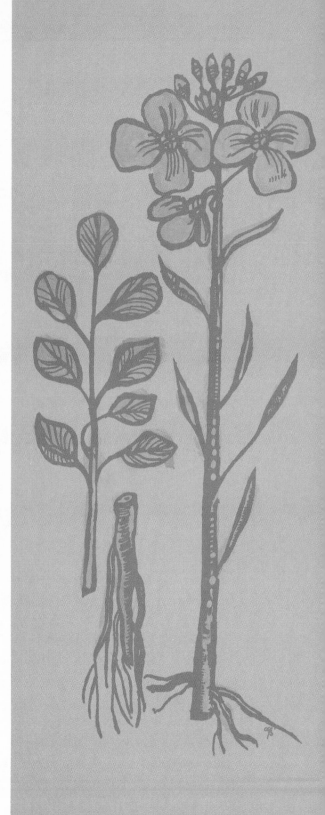

Who plants a garden builds
a carillon
To peal her praises with the
pulse of time
And laud her with the earth's
loveliest, lasting chime
In bright, unalterable antiphon

– LIAM BROPHY

A Mary Garden is a garden dedicated to Mary, the Mother of God. In a Mary Garden, which can be as small as a clay pot or as large as a city block, a statue of Mary is surrounded by herbs and flowers which have special significance for her, through legends or naming. A Mary Garden can be formal or wild, sunny or shady, indoors or out. It can contain annuals and perennials, herbs, ground covers and shrubs. It can be planted with bulbs to bloom in the early spring, plants that continue into the fall and evergreens that give color in winter.

Historians believe that the first gardens honoring Mary were cloister gardens in monasteries. These gardens did not survive, but there is archaeological and documentary evidence of their existence. Some of the first monastery gardens were built in the ruins of Roman villas and used existing walls for enclosures; they contained flowering plants and herbs used for medicinal purposes as well as vegetables and fruit trees.

For a time early Christianity banned the use of flowers for religious ceremonies because of their pagan associations and questioned the value of herbs for healing on the grounds that curing lay in the hands of God.

With the collapse of the western Roman Empire, flower and herb gardens virtually disappeared. Life was a struggle. But some monks kept their herb gardens and continued their devotion to Mary.

Around 520, Saint Benedict founded his order at Monte Cassino. His Black Monks became proficient in agriculture and horticulture and an example for their neighbors. Flowers were now grown to deck the altars in church and glorify God. The rose, lily and iris were considered especially appropriate for this purpose.

Saint Isidore of Seville (c. 560-636) wrote of a need for a garden at one end of the cloister in his monastery. And Saint Fiacre (600-670) included a garden in the monastery he founded in the seventh century near Meaux in France. That garden, surrounding an oratory and hospice he built and dedicated to Mary, may have been the model for Mary Gardens. A legend that his garden was miraculously enclosed and protected grew out of the fact that wild animals would not enter his garden because of his saintliness.

As devotion to Mary grew during the Middle Ages, the enclosed garden became a symbol for Mary's purity and artists depicted her in a garden, surrounded by the plants that represented her attributes. Today the faithful again honor Mary in gardens dedicated to her, filled with her flowers and herbs.

∽ Your Personal Mary Garden ∽

You can situate your personal Mary Garden in a secluded corner of your garden or backyard, or open it to the neighborhood in front of your house. You can put it on your windowsill or patio or on a table indoors.

Mary can be represented by a statue, a plaque, holy card or icon. Ann Duffy of Annapolis, Maryland, painted the likeness of Mary's face from a holy card on a piece of wood and waterproofed it for her outdoor garden. A large concrete statue of Mary, found in a garden ornaments shop, graces my Mary Garden.

The location, size and soil of the site will determine what you can plant in an outdoor garden. After that, personal preference (and sometimes divine providence), can guide you. Since the Mary names of hundreds of flowers and herbs have survived, your garden can contain many of your favorite flowers, planted with the intention of honoring Mary and representing her many attributes.

Fred Ward of East Falmouth, Massachusetts, wrote about his wild, inexpensive Mary Garden in a letter to the editor of the *New England Gardener*. He had planted rose of Sharon, hollyhocks, yellow daylilies and red roses around the edges of his plot when illness interfered. Unable to do any more, he waited to see what would come up and was "rewarded by a succession of vetch, clover, daisies, the lilies, Queen Anne's lace, and lots more...."

Gardening books can provide information about soil preparation and planting of seeds or plants. The five Mary Gardens described in this chapter are full of ideas about Mary's flowers and plants for various seasons, for herb gardens, ground covers, border edging and year-round color.

∽ Plants for the First-time Mary Gardener ∽

John Stokes, cofounder of Mary's Gardens Nursery, suggests the first-time Mary gardener select from the following list of well-known flowers which bear Mary names:

Marian Name	Common Name	Botanical Name
Annunciation Lily	Madonna lily	*Lilium candidum*
Eyes of Mary	Forget-me-not	*Myosotis* species
Mary-Loves	English daisy	*Bellis perennis*
Mary's Crown	Bachelor's-button	*Centauria cyannis*
Mary's Gold	Marigold	*Tagetes* species
Mary's Humility	Violet	*Viola odorata*
Mary's Prayer	Tulip	*Tulipa*
Mary's Rose	Rose	*Rosa* species
Mary's Shoes	Columbine	*Aquilegia vulgaris*
Mary's Star	Daffodil	*Narcissus pseudonarc.*
Mary's Sword of Sorrow	Iris	*Iris germanica*
Mary's Tears	Larkspur	*Consolida orientalis*
Mary's Tears	Lily of the valley	*Convallaria majalis*
Mother Love	Patient Lucy	*Impatiens wallerana*
Our Lady in the Shade	Love in a mist	*Nigella damascena*
Our Lady's Delight	Miniature pansy	*Viola tricolor*
Our Lady's Earrings	Garden balsam	*Impatiens balsaminum*
Our Lady's Mantle	Common morning-glory	*Ipomoea purpurea*
Our Lady's Pincushion	Sweet scabious	*Scabiosa atropurpurea*
Our Lady's Praises	Common petunia	*Petunia hybrida*
The Virgin	Common zinnia	*Zinnia elegens*

∾ Plants for a Herbal Mary Garden ∾

A herb garden might include some of the following:

Marian Name	Common Name	Botanical Name
Heavenly Way	Common chicory	*Cichorium intybus*
Herb of Grace	Common rue	*Ruta graveolens*
Holy Communion plant	Common basil	*Ocimum basilicum*
Mary's Bedstraw	Creeping thyme	*Thymus praecox*
Mary's Bedstraw	Marjoram	*Origanum vulgare*
Mary's Bitter Sorrow	Common dandelion	*Taraxacum officinale*
Mary's Drying Plant	Lavender	*Lavandula officinalis*
Mary's Plant	German chamomile	*Matricaria recutita*
Mary's Shawl	Common sage	*Salvia officinalis*
Mother of God's Flower	Sweet marjoram	*Origanum majorana*
Our Lady's Duster	Lovage	*Levisticum officinale*
Our Lady's Milkwort	Bethlehem sage	*Pulmonaria saccharata*
Our Lady's Mint	Spearmint	*Mentha spicata*
Our Lady's Little Vine	Parsley	*Petroselinum crispum*
The Virgin's Humility	Common thyme	*Thymus vulgaris*

∾ Indoor Mary Gardens ∾

Bonnie Roberson, pioneer in developing variations in Mary Gardens, created indoor gardens for the blind, sick and shut-in, but indoor gardens can also be used by those without garden space or those in colder climates who want to honor Mary during the winter months.

These gardens were often designed around a theme, such as the Japanese Madonna and Child or Mexican Nativity Scene. The Madonna Shrine was in a fishbowl, and Madonnas were often surrounded by plants in a brandy snifter or tall glass.

Our Lady of Zapopan, Mexico, was surrounded by aloe, agape and various

cacti including Easter cactus and Lady's Finger Cactus. A Hummel Madonna was surrounded by miniature box (Purification Flower), Kenilworth ivy (Tears of Mary), baby's tears, creeping fig (Flight into Egypt) and Joseph's coat (*Alternanthera ficoidea*).

Roberson, who did extensive research on tropical and sub-tropical plants, suggested some of them for indoor gardens. Among them:

Marian Name	Common Name	Botanical Name
Angel's Wings	Fancy-leaved caladium	*Caladium hortulanum*
Beautiful Lady	Geranium	*Pelargonium domest.*
Lady Palm	Lady palm	*Rhapis excelsa*
Lady's Eardrops	Hardy fuchsia	*Fuchsia magellanica*
Lady's Finger	Golden-star cactus	*Mammillaria elongata.*
Lady's Fringe	Star begonia	*Begonia heracleifolia*
Lady's Hair	Maidenhair fern	*Adiantum tenerum*
Lady's Slipper	Lady-slipper	*Paphiopedilum* species
Lady's Slipper	Pocketbook flower	*Calceolaria herbeohybr.*
Madonna	Garden African violet	*Saintpaulia ionantha*
Maiden's Hair	Asparagus fern	*Asparagus setaceus*
Mary's Bouquet	Rosemary	*Rosmarinus officinalis*
Mary's Gold	Rosary plant	*Crassula rupestris*
Mary's Hair	Strawberry geranium	*Saxifraga stolonifera*
Mary's Heart	Begonia	*Begonia fuchsioides*
Mary's Purity	Jasmine	*Jasminum officinale*
Mary's Thorn	Miniature rose	*Rosa* hybrids
Virginity	Myrtle	*Vinca minor*

❧ Five Mary Gardens ❧

Five large Mary Gardens, each with an original statue of the Madonna and all connected with religious institutions, are located east of the Mississippi River. To walk through the gardens is to take a sensual and spiritual tour. We smile at Our Lady's Delight, smell the fragrant lavender with its tiny florets and imagine Mary's purse spilling forth marigolds. Thyme and bedstraw, violets and columbine all tell of Mary's life and inspire us to prayer and meditation.

Woods Hole, Massachusetts

The Garden of Our Lady, across Millfield Street from St. Joseph Church in Woods Hole on Cape Cod, Massachusetts, grows behind a six-foot tall yew hedge. Yew is the Tree of the Cross. A short wooden gate in the middle of the hedge invites us to "Please enter and close the gate." Entering, we find the bell tower to the right and the Mary Garden to the left. To the right of the bell tower is St. Joseph's Garden, where plants with St. Joseph names and other religious names grow.

A wide grassy passage leads from the bell tower to the Mary Garden. As we approach the garden we see a slate marker on the ground before us; etched on it are the words: "Attend to this sacred place." As we move along the passage we begin to reflect on Mary's life and we know this is a sacred place. There is a stillness here, alongside the quiet waters of Eel Pond, and the sounds of the nearby street are muffled. We see the Mary statue in the middle of the garden and we enter her place. It is the "garden enclosed" of medieval times.

To the right of the entrance a wooden information box contains the garden plan and list of plants, with their Marian and botanical names, so that visitors may identify the various plants and flowers. A symphony of color greets us, plants and blossoms of various shapes and sizes and heights waving in the breeze and clamoring for the sun. The mood is peaceful and prayerful. On the left is the soft green of the yew hedge; to the right a low stockade fence separates the garden from the edge of Eel Pond, where moored boats float quietly.

Our eyes are immediately drawn to Vinol M. S. Hannell's sculpture of Mary, standing tall above the sword-like iris leaves and the waving branches of old rose bushes gone wild and threatening to envelop it. Both the white Japanese iris and the rose are known as Her Flower. Called "The Virgin," the concrete statue depicts Mary as she might have appeared at the moment of the annunciation. It was designed to weather slowly and has resisted the elements well. Rain, snow and salt have not changed the details of Mary's face and the statue looks much like it did more than sixty years ago. The humble and serene expression on Mary's face is reflected in the unpretentious, tranquil garden.

When the church celebrated its hundredth anniversary in 1982, the garden was restored to its 1937 plan by Jane McLaughlin, a parishioner who was writing a history of the parish for the centennial.

Annapolis, Maryland

The Mary Garden at St. Mary's Church, Annapolis, Maryland, is located behind the church in the quadrangle formed by the church, the rectory and the historic John Carroll House. St. Mary's Church, on narrow Duke of Gloucester Street in the heart of old Annapolis, stands on the site of the first private Catholic chapel in Maryland, built in 1822 by Charles Carroll.

The garden features two very old crepe myrtle trees and hundred-year-old boxwood bushes (Candlemas greens) circling an area where schoolchildren

plant their own garden each spring, each child naming her plant for her mother. In front of the boxwood circle a wooden box lists the plants growing here and their Marian names.

In an area named the Rosary a variety of rose bushes (Her Flower) have been planted. In the herb garden, an angel watches over the Herb of Grace (rue) and other herbs, planted in a geometric design. Mary's apple tree (Lady Apple) grows in an area called Marie's Garden.

At the end of the garden is the Mary of Nazareth statue, designed by Leo Irrerra and sculpted from polished Vermont granite. Mary stands with one arm around Jesus, who looks up at her. Our Blessed Mother's expression is one of love and concern and she holds his hand protectively. Three heart-shaped basins at the base of the statue form a circulating pool.

Dayton, Ohio

The Mary Garden at Our Lady of Lourdes Grotto on the property of Mount Saint John is near Dayton, Ohio. Marian vines and perennial flowers cling to the craggy slopes of the grotto, a proportional model of the Lourdes Grotto at Massabielle in France. Waterfalls cascade down tufa rock into a fish pond and

rock garden. Colorful annuals, all with Mary names, are planted at the feet of a statue of Our Lady of Lourdes which sits high up in a recess of the grotto.

In the center an alcove shelters an altar and candles burn continuously. Pots of flowers have been placed there by those who come to pray. A bench in front of this space invites meditation; other benches are placed further back. One or more persons silent in prayer or meditation are often found here.

In front of the grotto there is room for the faithful to gather for liturgy or the rosary. Giant evergreens grow behind and to each side of the grotto.

Portage, Michigan

The Mary Garden at St. Catherine of Siena Church runs along the front of the church, high on a hill. Both church and garden can be seen from the road. The sun beats down on the garden most of the day, and the many-colored plants and blossoms form a cool oasis.

In the garden, a brick walk curves between planted areas, divides to surround an oval bed and continues to the right where it surrounds a circular bed. Numerous evergreen shrubs, most with Mary names, provide color throughout the year and form a backdrop for sun-loving Mary flowers. Low wooden markers announce each plant.

Approaching Mary's statue on the left we see white popcorn roses, reminding us of the virginal rose, "The rose wherein the Divine Word was made incarnate." Created by sculptor Gerald Westgerdes and cast in bronze, the statue represents Mary, Model of the Church. She is "with child" and "in anguish for delivery." Satan in the form of an ancient sea monster confronts her, waiting to devour her child, but she rests on the earth which saves her by surrounding her with flowers. In front of the statue grows the Dragon's Blood of genus *Sedum*.

Across the walk from the statue a three-sided lattice-work enclosure and two benches encourage private meditation.

Cincinnati, Ohio

The Mary Garden at the Episcopal Convent of the Transfiguration is located on a shady hillside on the grounds of the convent in suburban Glendale. This tranquil Mary Garden is filled with shade-loving plants and surrounds a statue of the Madonna and Child which was placed there sometime in the 1960's.

A concrete walkway slopes gently downhill from the entrance, leading to a gazebo on the left and a rock garden on the right. Along the path thirteen large shade trees, mostly sugar maples interspersed among elm, oak, locust, hackberry and ash, provide cool refuge on a hot summer day.

Water flows through the rock garden and into a pond at a lower level. The

Virgin Flower (vinca) and Where God Has Walked (ground ivy) cover the rocks. A walk leads to the Madonna statue ahead and a bench invites the visitor to sit awhile. The statue depicts Mary cradling the infant Jesus with her right arm. Her left hand is raised toward her shoulder, as if preparing  to give something to Jesus, whose arm reaches toward her hand. To the right are a small bird bath and a plaque with the inscription:

> This Garden is dedicated to the Blessed Virgin Mary and called by Her name in accordance with a tradition in the Church dating from the 15th century and the rise of Monasticism. Such gardens were used by the monks as a means of teaching the unlettered members of their flocks to pray and meditate on the life of Our Lord, His blessed Mother and the early saints.
>
> May we, too, use this garden to God's praise and Glory.

∽ Blessing the Mary Garden ∽

In medieval times it was customary to bless gardens and fields as holy places and this practice has continued to this day. The blessing may include a plea for a good harvest as well as a prayer of thanksgiving for the garden and plants.

On August 15, the Feast of the Assumption, it is customary, especially in rural areas, to bless plants which are then brought home by the faithful for religious use. On this day the first fruits of healing and life-sustaining herbs, grains and other plants are brought to Mass by the faithful tied in "Assumption Bundles" and carried to the altar in procession. After the blessing they are brought home to be treated with reverence as holy objects.

While it has been the custom to have a priest bless a garden and other objects, the blessing may be given by anyone who has the intention of calling God's blessings on the garden. A blessing can include a prayer of praise for God's work, thanksgiving for his gifts and a request for future blessings and gifts. Some examples of blessings follow.

From the *Rural Life Prayerbook* of the National Catholic Rural Life Conference comes this blessing, taken from the Roman rite of the Catholic Church, for the Feast of the Assumption:

Almighty and everlasting God...with mind and word we earnestly implore your unspeakable Goodness to bless these various herbs and fruits, and add to their natural powers the grace of your new blessing. May they ward off disease and adversity from men and beasts who use them in your name.

The Servite Fathers use this prayer to bless flowers for Mary's Coronation (May crowning) on Holy Saturday:

O almighty everlasting God, we beseech thee to bless these flowers...that there may be in them goodness, virtue, tranquility, peace, victory, abundance of good things, the plenitude of blessing, thanksgiving to God the Father and the Son and the Holy Ghost, and a most pleasing commemoration of the glorious Mother of God—that...they may put forth an odor of virtue and sweetness.

This prayer is from the Dominican rite for the blessing of roses:

God...bless with your holy blessing these roses we offer to you this day...as a token of thanksgiving to you and of love and reverence for the ever blessed Virgin Mary of the Rosary. Do you, who have bestowed them as an odor of sweetness for our use and the easing of our ills, pour forth upon them heavenly blessing...that to whomsoever they may be brought in sickness may be healed.

The Mary Garden may be blessed with a universal blessing used for any object or with a blessing used for religious statues of Jesus, Mary and the saints, as in the following prayer from the Roman rite:

Almighty and eternal God...as often as we look on this image with our bodily eyes, so often do we consider the actions of your saints with our mind's eye, and ponder their sanctity for our imitation. Be so good, we beg of you, to bless and sanctify this statue...that whoever in the presence of this image humbly pays devout reverence and honor to your only-begotten Son and his Blessed Mother, may through their merits and intercession win grace in this life, and everlasting glory in the world to come.

The Mary Garden may also be blessed as a holy place on the Feast of the Nativity of Mary, September 8, the traditional day for the liturgical blessing of seeds, flowers and crops for the coming year.

Aue fancta parens e
nixa puerpera regem q̃
celum terramq; regit
in fecula feculoꝝ. ꝓs Sentiant
omnes tuũ leuamen quicuq; ce
lebrant tuam commemoratio
nem. Gloꝛia patri et filio et fpi
ritui fancto. ficut erat in pꝛinci

Appendix

Lilies for her purity,
Blue bells and morning glories for
    the cloak she wore;
Baby's Breath for the Child she nurtured,
And for her willing feet the Lady Slipper;
Foxglove to warm her gentle hands,
Sweet Woodruff (Bedstraw) for her rest.

— AUTHOR UNKNOWN

Our Lady, known as the "Flower of the Field," is said to be symbolized by all flowers. There may be more truth than legend to this belief, since there are at least a thousand flowers and herbs named after Mary. More than six hundred are listed in *Mariana 1*, based on research by Winifred Jellife Emerson and John S. Stokes, Jr. Additional species appear in *Tropical and Semi-Tropical Trees, Shrubs and Plants with Religious Names*, based on research by Bonnie Roberson.

The plant names and religious associations were drawn from more than a hundred general, horticultural, folklore and dialect dictionaries, horticultural listings and books of religious legends and customs. Marian names of flowers have been found in all the countries of Christendom, with some names unique to one or two countries and others, such as the rose, lily and milk-thistle, found in most or all.

This appendix lists more than two hundred Marian names for flowers and herbs. As with the flower legends, some flowers have several names while the same name or attribute is associated with several flowers. Additional information about the naming is provided when available.

The current botanical name for each plant is listed. In some cases the plant was known by a botanical name which has now been assigned to a different genus. Some plants, unfortunately, such as the *Fagonia* and the Virgin's Smile, could not be included as the present genus could not be found.

The flowers have been arranged in groups for ease in locating certain collections of flowers, such as those associated with her life, her features or her garments. Each cluster may also be used as a guide to meditation about Mary or in creating a Mary Garden.

᪥ Mary's Attributes ᪥

BEAUTIFUL LADY—(*Atropa belladonna*) Belladonna. From the Spanish.

BLESSED MARY—(*Convallaria var.*) Lily of the valley. In Spanish, *Beata Maria.*

DEAR MOTHER'S LOVE—(*Thymus vulgaris*) Wild thyme.

DEAR MOTHER'S LOVE— (*Impatiens wallerana*) Patient Lucy. From Poland.

FAITH PLANT—(*Trifolium incarnatum*) Crimson clover. From Spain.

FRUITFUL VIRGIN—(*Fragaria vesca*) Strawberry. Symbol of Mary's fruitfulness, since it bears flowers and fruit at the same time.

HERB OF GRACE—(*Ruta graveolens*) Rue. Named from the use of its branches in blessing the faithful with holy water.

LADY MARY—(*Pelargonium limoneum*) Lemon geranium.

LADY'S HOPE—(*Trifolium agrarium*) Yellow clover.

LITTLE MARY—(*Zinnia peruviana: multiflora*) Zinnia.

LILY OF THE VALLEY— (*Convallaria majalis*) Also called ladder to heaven. Symbol of humility; tiny bell-shaped white flowers humbly bend downward.

MADONNA IRIS—(*Iris florentina*) Iris, the royal lily, is an emblem of Mary's queenship and of her descent from the royal house of David.

MADONNA LILY—(*Lilium candidum*) Virgin lily. An ancient emblem of our Lady: The waxy white petals symbolize her bodily purity and the gold anthers her purity of soul.

MAIDEN PINK—(*Dianthus deltoides*) In England, gillyflower.

MARY'S CROWN—(*Centaurea cyanus*) Cornflower, bachelor's-button.

MARY'S FLOWER OF GOD—(*Bellis perennis*) English daisy, innocence.

MARY'S GLORY—(*Hypericum perforatum*) Saint-John's-wort.

MARY'S GOLD—(*Calendula offici-nalis*) Marigold. Representatitve of Mary's glory, in heaven and on earth.

MARY'S HAND OF PITY—(*Orchis var.*) Wild purple orchid. Also called Christ's Blood and Gethsemani. In Gaelic, *Magairlin Meidhreach.*

MARY'S HEART—(*Dicentra spectabilis*) Bleeding-heart. Each heart-shaped bloom has at its base a red and white droplet, signifying the blood and water flowing from Christ's pierced side.

MARY'S HELP—(*Erica carnea*) Snow heather.

MARY'S PURITY—(*Rosa species*) White rose.

MARY'S RADIANCE—(*Ranunculus aconitifolius*) White buttercup. Represents stars from heaven coming to earth to honor Mary and her child.

MARY'S TULIP—(*Tulipa clusiana*) Lady tulip. A symbol of spiritual openness.

MARY'S VIRTUES—(*Lagenaria siceraria*) White-flowered gourd.

MOTHER OF THOUSANDS—(*Mentha Requienii*) Spanish moss. Creeping herb.

MOTHER OF THOUSANDS—(*Saxifraga stolinofera sarmentosa*) Strawberry geranium.

MYSTIC ROSE—(*Rosa species*) Rose. Dante called Mary the "Mystical Rose."

OUR LADY'S FAITH—(*Veronica maritima*) Veronica.

OUR LADY'S KEYS—(*Primula veris*) Cowslip. Clusters of bright golden or light yellow flowers suggest a bunch of keys, representing the keys of Mary Mediatrix to the storehouses of heavenly grace.

OUR LADY'S MODESTY—(*Viola odorata*) Sweet violet. So named because of the "modest" manner in which the blooms nestle among the leaves. Violets are associated with our Lady as an emblem of her humility in religious paintings.

OUR LADY'S PRAISES—(*Petunia hybrida*) Blue and white petunia.

PURITY OF MARY—(*Leontopodium alpinum*) Edelweiss.

ROSE OF JERICHO—(*Rosa centifolia*) Cabbage rose. From Spain.

ROSE OF SHARON—(*Anemone coronaria*) Lily-of-the-field. In biblical times, various flowers were known as lilies of the field and the rose of Sharon.

ROSE OF SHARON—(*Crocus vernus*) Spring crocus. Rose comes from a Hebrew word whose root means "bulb-like" and applies to many flowers.

ROSE OF SHARON—(*Hypericum calycinum*) Mary was said to be the "Rose of Sharon" of the Song of Solomon.

SAINT MARY—(*Chrysanthemum Parthenium*) Feverfew. *Santa Maria* in Spanish.

SAINT MARY'S HOLLY—(*Ilex opaca, var.*) Christmas holly. Said to symbolize the constant virginity of Mary.

SWEET MARY—(*Centranthus ruber*)
Red valerian. From England.
SWEET MARY—(*Melissa officinalis*)
Lemon balm.
SWEET MARY—(*Monarda didyma*)
Bee balm.
THE VIRGIN'S FLOWER—(*Vinca minor*) Periwinkle. Mentioned in Chaucer's poems.

THE VIRGIN'S HUMILITY—
(*Thymus vulgaris*) Wild thyme.
VIRGIN PINK—(*Dianthus plumarius*)
Clove pink.
VIRGIN STOCK—(*Malcolmia maritima*) Virginia stock.

∞ Mary's Life ∞

ASSUMPTION LILY—(*Hosta plantaginea*) Plantain lily. Blooms at the time of the Feast of the Assumption.
BETHLEHEM STAR—(*Campanula fragilis*) Bellflower.
CHRISTMAS FLOWER—(*Euphorbia pulcherrima*) Poinsettia or Christmas star. In Spanish, called the *Flor de Noche Buena*.
CHRISTMAS HOLLY—(*Ilex opaca*) American holly.
CHRISTMAS ORCHID—(*Cattleya trianaei*) Winter orchid. Variety *Mariae* has silvery-white petals veined with pink, lip is deep magenta-crimson.
CHRISTMAS STARWORT—(*Aster grandiflorus*) Aster.
EPIPHANY FLOWER—
(*Chrysanthemum indicum*)
Chrysanthemum.
FLIGHT INTO EGYPT—(*Acer pseudoplatanus*) Sycamore.
The Holy Family rested under a giant sycamore during the Flight into Egypt.

FLIGHT INTO EGYPT—(*Ficus carica*) Fig tree. Legend says that the Holy Family ate the fruit of this tree during their flight into Egypt.
HEAVENLY WAY—(*Cichorium intybus*) Chicory.
HOLY NIGHT ROSE—(*Helleborus niger*) Christmas rose. Legend that it bloomed on the night that Jesus was born.
INCARNATION—(*Gladiolus hybrids*)
Gladiolus.
LADY'S BEDSTRAW—(*Dianthus carthusianorum*) Clustered pink. Mary used bedstraw to prepare a bed for Jesus.
LILY OF NAZARETH—(*Lilium Martagon*) Martagon lily.
MADONNA'S JUNIPER BUSH—
(*Juniperus*) Juniper. Legend that it sheltered the Holy Family during the flight into Egypt.

MARY'S BEDSTRAW—Several vari-
eties have borne this name:
(*Dryopteris felix-mas*) wood fern;
(*Epilobium angustifolium*) fireweed;
(*Origanum vulgare*) marjoram;
(*Trifolium repens*) white clover;
Mary used various bedstraws to
prepare a bed for Jesus.

MARY'S BITTER SORROW—
(*Taraxacum officinale*) Common
dandelion. Bitterness symbolizes
the depth of Mary's sorrow.

MARY'S DELIGHT—(*Viola alba*)
White violet. White with violet
center and veins. Sweet scented.

MARY'S GLORIES—(*Rosa species*)
Gold rose.

MARY'S MAYFLOWER—(*Crataegus
monogyna*) English hawthorn. First
blossoms at the Nativity, bears
fruit and blossoms again in Mary's
month of May, with second crop
of fruit appearing around the time
of Mary's birthday, September 8.

MARY'S PURIFICATION—
(*Potentilla recta*) Cinquefoil.

MARY'S SORROWS—(*Cyclamen
europaeum purpurascens*) Bleeding
nun.

MARY'S SORROWS—(*Rosa species*)
Red rose.

MARY'S STAR—(*Campanula isophyl-
la*) Italian bellflower, star-of-
Bethlehem.

MARY'S STAR—(*Chrysanthemum
leucanthemum*) Oxeye daisy.
Legend says that it bloomed in
front of the manger when Christ
was born.

MARY'S STAR—(*Narcissus
pseudonarcissus*) Daffodil.

MARY'S SWORD OF SORROW—
(*Iris germanica*) German flag iris.
Sword-like foliage recalls the
prophecy of Simon to Mary at the
Presentation of Jesus that Mary's
soul would be pierced by a sword.

MARY'S TEARS—(*Chiococca alba*)
Snowberry. From Latin America.

MARY'S TEARS—(*Delphinium ajacis*)
Larkspur.

MARY'S TEARS—(*Lithospermum
officinale*) Gromwell. Greenish-
white flowers remind one of tears.
From Germany.

MARY'S THORN—(*Rosa canina*)
Dog rose. From Germany.

MARY'S THORN—(*Rosa Eglanteria*)
Eglantine rose. From Germany.

MOTHER OF GOD'S SORROWS—
(*Samolus valerandi*) Brookweed.
In Spanish, *Ansiam de la Mare
de Dieu.*

OUR LADY'S BIRTHDAY
FLOWER—(*Aster amellus*) Italian
aster. Named because it blooms
around the time of the Feast of the
Nativity of our Lady, September 8.

OUR LADY'S BIRTHDAY
FLOWER—(*Mentha Pulegium*)
Pennyroyal.

OUR LADY'S DELIGHT—(*Viola tricolor*) Pansy or Johnny-jump-up.
From French *pensee*, meaning
"thoughts."

OUR LADY'S MILK HERB—
(*Pulmonaria officinalis*) Blue lungwort. English legend that the
leaves became white-spotted when
our Lady's breast milk fell on
them.

OUR LADY'S RESTING PLACE—
(*Veronica chamaedrys, semi-dwarf*)
Germander Speedwell. Blossomed
where Mary rested on the flight
into Egypt.

OUR LADY'S RUE—(*Thalictrum
clavatum*) Lady rue.

OUR LADY'S RUE—(*Thalictrum
dipterocarpum*) Meadow rue. Also
known as Our Lady of the
Meadow. Associated with sorrow
and mourning, possibly because of
the purple color of the flowers.

OUR LADY'S TEARS—(*Coix lacry-
ma-jobi*) Job's tears. Tear-like large,
hard, shiny pearly-white to gray
seed pods. From Spain.

OUR LADY'S TEARS—(*Convallariia
majalis*) Lily of the valley. Tiny
white nodding bell-shaped flowers
can be likened to a train of tears.

OUR LADY'S TEARS—
(*Tradescantia*) Spiderwort. Named
from the blue drop of liquid emit-
ted from each spent bloom and
resting on the supporting foliage.

OUR LADY'S TRESSES—
(*Spiranthes cernua*) Common
ladies'-tresses. The legend holds
that at the foot of the cross, Mary,
in deep agony, tore out a tress of
her hair which Saint John preserved.

OUR LADY'S WEDDING—(*Phlox
divaricata*) Wild sweet william.
Blossoms were used in garlands
and crowns in medieval England.

PARADISE FLOWER—(*Acacia
greggii*) Texas mimosa.

PURIFICATION PLANT—(*Buxus
sempervirens*) Boxwood. Mary
went to the Temple for a ritual
purification ceremony thirty days
after Jesus' birth.

QUEEN'S TEARS—(*Billbergia
nutans*) Friendship plant. From
tropical America.

SAINT MARY'S HOLLY—(*Ilex
crenata*) Box-leaved holly. In Spain
and Italy, known as wild myrtle
and found in Christmas cribs.

STAR OF BETHLEHEM—(*Stellaria
holostea*) Greater stitchwort. From
England.

STAR OF BETHLEHEM—
(*Tragopogon porrifolius*) Salsify.
From England.

TEARS OF MARY—(*Cymbalaria
muralis*) Kenilworth ivy.

THE VIRGIN'S TEARS—(*Allium
roseum*) Onion. In Spanish,
Lagrimas de la Virgen.

VIRGIN BIRTH—(*Prunus
amygdalus*) Almond.

VISITATION—(*Rosa species*)
Red and white roses.

BLUE-EYED MARY—(*Collinsia verna*) Blue-eyed Mary, innocence. The round, eye-like whorls of blue and white blooms remind one of eyes.

BLUE-EYED MARY—(*Sisyrinchium angustifolium*) Blue-eyed grass. The bright blue flowers are suggestive of eyes.

EYES OF MARY—(*Myosotis scorpioides*) Forget-me-not. Small, dainty blue blossoms suggestive of eyes.

GOLDEN MAIDENHAIR—(*Polypodium vulgare*) Wall fern. From England.

LADY BEAUTIFUL—(*Perlargonium domesticum*) Geranium.

LADY'S FINGERS—(*Arum maculatum*) Cuckoopint. From England.

LADY'S FINGERS AND THUMBS—(*Lotus corniculatus*) Bird's-foot trefoil. From England.

LADY'S NAVEL—(*Umbilicus rupestris*) Navelwort. From England.

MADONNA'S MILK—(*Lamium album*) White dead nettle. From England.

MARY'S FIVE FINGERS—(*Potentilla reptans*) Creeping cinquefoil. In Gaelic, *Cuig Mhear Mhuire.*

MARY'S HAND OF PITY—(*Potentilla nepalensis*) Five-finger. Named from the hand-like appearance of its white roots when it is lifted from the soil.

MARY'S HAIR—(*Ranunculus species, yellow*) Wood Goldilocks. In Gaelic, *Gruaig Mhuire.*

MARY'S TRESSES—(*Spiranthes cernua*) Nodding ladies' tresses. Named from the sprial of its flower heads reminiscent of plaited hair. In Gaelic, *Cuilin Mhuire.*

OUR LADY'S FINGERS—(*Anthyllis vulneraria*) Kidney vetch. Clustered florets remind one of fingers. In Gaelic, *Meoir Mhuire.*

OUR LADY'S FINGERS—(*Digitalis purpurea*) Common foxglove. In Normandy and Brittany, France, known as the Virgin's Fingers (*Doigts de la Vierge*) or Our Lady's Fingers (*Les Doigtiers de Notre Dame*).

OUR LADY'S FINGERS—(*Lonicera caprifolium*) Honeysuckle. Clusters of finger-like buds remind one of fingers.

OUR LADY'S FINGERS—(*Stachys species*) Betony. From Germany.

OUR LADY'S HAIR—(*Adiantum capillus-veneris*) Maidenhair fern, Venushair. In England often used to decorate the altars for the Feast of Corpus Christi.

OUR LADY'S HAIR—(*Briza media*) Quaking grass. From England.

OUR LADY'S MILK DROPS—(*Silybum marianum*) St. Mary's Thistle. From England.

OUR LADY'S THISTLE, LADY
MILK—(*Carduus Marianus*)
Plumeless thistle. From England.

OUR LADY'S THUMB—(*Polygonum
species*) Knotweed. Includes
shrubs, garden plants, weeds given
this name in old botanical and
herbal dictionaries. Named from
the characteristic thumb-print like
mark on each leaf.

OUR LADY'S TRESSES—(*Briza
maxima*) Quaking grass. Plant
showers drooping, braid-like
spikelets of seeds.

SAINT MARY'S HAND—(*Leonurus
Cardiaca*) Motherwort. From
Spain, *Mano de Santa Maria*.

VIRGIN'S MILK—(*Ornithogalum
umbellatum*) Star of Bethlehem.
In Spanish, *Leche de Virgen*.

⊷ *Mary's Garments* ⊶

LADY FRINGE—(*Begonia
heracleifolia*) Star begonia.
From tropical America.

LADY'S BOOTS—(*Lotus
corniculatus*) Bird's-foot trefoil.
From England.

LADY'S BUTTONS—(*Stellaria
holostea*) Greater stitchwort.
From England.

LADY'S CHEMISE—(*Stellaria
holostea*) Greater stitchwort.
From England.

LADY'S CLOAK—(*Cardamine
pratensis*) Lady's-smock.
From England.

LADY'S FLANNEL—(*Verbascum
thapsus*) Flannel plant, mullein.
Named from the hairy, flannel-like
texture of the leaves. From
England.

LADY'S GARTERS—(*Phalaris
arundinacea var. picta*) Gardener's-
garters. From England.

LADY'S GLOVE—(*Lotus
corniculatus*) Bird's-foot trefoil.
From England.

LADY'S GLOVE—(*Cardamine
pratensis*) Lady's smock.
From England.

LADY'S LACES—(*Phalaris
arundinacea picta*) Ribbon grass.
From England.

LADY'S MANTLE—(*Cardamine
pratensis*) Lady's-smock.
From England.

LADY'S NIGHTCAP—(*Calystgegia
sepium*) Wild morning glory,
Bindweed. From England.

LADY'S NIGHTCAP—(*Campanula
medium*) Canterbury-bells.
From England.

LADY'S PURSES—(*Caldeolaria
species*) Pocketbook flower.
From England.

LADY'S SHOE—(*Adlumia fungosa*)
Fumitory. From England.

LADY'S SLIPPER—(*Arum maculatum*)
Cuckoopint. From England.

LADY'S SLIPPER—(*Cytisus
scoparius*) Scotch broom.
From the United Kingdom.

LADY'S SLIPPER—(both *Paphiopedilum* and *Phragmipedium* species) Lady-slipper. From tropical America.

LADY'S SLIPPER—(*Ranunculus acris*) Tall buttercup. From England.

LADY'S SMOCK—(*Calystgegia sepium*) Wild morning glory, Bindweed. From England.

LADY'S SMOCK—(*Cardamine pratensis*) Lady's smock. In Gaelic, *Leine Mhuire*.

LADY'S WHITE PETTICOAT— (*Stellaria holostea*) Greater stitchwort. From England.

MANTLE OF THE QUEEN— (*Xanthosoma sagittifolium*) Malanga. From the West Indies.

MARY'S MANTLE—(*Alchemilla vulgaris*) Lady's-mantle. From Germany. In Gaelic, *Bratog Mhuire*.

MARY'S RUFFLES—(*Narcissus pseudonarcissus*) Daffodil. Rows of wavy blossom petals resemble ruffles. From France and England.

MARY'S SHAWL—(*Salvia officinalis*) Common sage.

MARY'S SLIPPER—(*Aconitum napellus*) Helmet flower, Monk's hood. Florets resemble a monk's hood or a slipper.

MOTHER OF GOD'S MANTLE— (*Petasites species*) Butterbur. In Spanish, *Mantell de la Mere de Dios*.

MOTHER OF GOD'S SLIPPERS— (*Calceolaria species*) Slipper flower. In Spanish, *Sabatetas de la Mare de Deu*.

MOTHER OF GOD'S SLIPPERS— (*Ophrys apifera*) Bee orchid. In Spanish, *Sabatetas de la Mare de Deu*.

OUR LADY'S DUSTER—(*Levisticum officinale*) Lovage. Fragrant herb.

OUR LADY'S EARDROPS—(*Fuchsia species*) Garden fuchsia. Pendant, earring-like blossoms.

OUR LADY'S EARRINGS— (*Impatiens balsamina*) Garden balsam. Earring-like rosette blossoms clustered close to shoots.

OUR LADY'S FLANNEL—(*Echium vulgare*) Viper's bugloss. Named from hairy, flannel-like texture of leaves.

OUR LADY'S FRILLS—(*Primula vulgaris*) Primrose. From Germany.

OUR LADY'S FRINGES— (*Gentianopsis species*) Fringed gentian. Also called Holy Name of Mary. Used to decorate altars on Feast of Nativity of Our Lady in Europe.

OUR LADY'S GLOVE—(*Digitalis purpurea*) Common foxglove. In French, *Gant de Notre Dame*. Blossoms in thin tall spires resemble fingers of gloves.

OUR LADY'S LACE—(*Petroselinum crispum*) Wild parsley. Flower of the Ascension.

OUR LADY'S MANTLE— (*Alchimella species*) Lady's-mantle. Named from the shape of the leaves. From Mexico.

OUR LADY'S MANTLE—(*Colocasia antiquorum*) Elephant's-ear. From tropical America and Spain. *Manto de Nostra Senora* in Spanish.

OUR LADY'S MANTLE—(*Ipomoea purpurea*) Common morning-glory. Mantle-like covering of leaves interspersed with intensely colored purple, blue or pink morning-blooming flowers.

OUR LADY'S MANTLE— (*Matricaria recutita*) Sweet false chamomile. Sweet-scented, many-branched, covers like a cloak. From Germany.

OUR LADY'S NIGHTCAP— (*Campanula medium*) Canterbury bells. Bell-shaped flowers resemble winter nightcaps.

OUR LADY'S PETTICOAT— (*Anemone nemorosa*) European wood anemone. Solitary white or purplish flowers resemble petticoats hanging out to dry. From England.

OUR LADY'S SHOE—(*Anthyllis vulneraria*) Kidney betch. From Germany.

OUR LADY'S SHOES—(*Aquilegia vulgaris*) Columbine. Fallen columbine spurs resemble shoes.

OUR LADY'S SLIPPER—(*Aquilegia vulgaris*) Columbine. Fallen spurs resemble slippers.

OUR LADY'S SLIPPER— (*Cypripedium calceolus*) Lady's slipper orchid.

OUR LADY'S SLIPPER—(*Impatiens balsamina*) Garden balsam.

OUR LADY'S SLIPPER—(*Polygala paucifolia*) Fringed milkwort.

OUR LADY'S SMOCK— (*Convolvulus arvensis*) Field bindweed. These small blooms are popular in rock gardens. From England.

OUR LADY'S VEIL—(*Gypsophila paniculata*) Baby's breath.

QUEEN'S MANTLE—(*Caladium, bicolor*) Angel-wings.

THE QUEEN'S SLIPPER— (*Centrosema virginianum*) Butterfly pea. From tropical America.

THE VIRGIN'S CUFF—(*Ipomoea alba*) Moonflower. From tropical America.

THE VIRGIN'S MANTLE— (*Ipomoea, tricolor*) Morning-glory. From tropical America.

THE VIRGIN'S SHOES—(*Clitoria ternatea*) Butterfly pea. From tropical America.

THE VIRGIN'S SHOES—(*Lonicera periclymenum*) Woodbine. In Spanish, *Zapatilla de la Virgen*.

In Mary's Household

CHRISTMAS CANDLE—(*Cassia alata*) Candlestick senna. From tropical America.

INFANT JESUS' PANTS AND SHIRTS—(*Adlumia fungosa*) Fumitory. In Spanish, *Panalitos y Camistas del Nino Jesus*.

INFANT JESUS' SHOES—
(*Antirrhinum majus*) Common
snapdragon. In Spanish, *Zapaticos
del Nino Jesus.*

LADY CAKES—(*Oxalis acetosella*)
European wood sorrel. From
England.

LADY'S BRUSHES—(*Dipsacus
fullonum*) Wild teasel. From
England.

LADY'S CUSHION—(*Anthyllis
vulneraria*) Kidney vetch. From
England.

LADY'S CUSHION—(*Centaurea
nigra*) Spanish-buttons. From
England.

LADY'S FEATHERBEDS—
(*Saxifraga granulata*) Meadow
saxifrage. From England.

LADY'S HATPINS—(*Knautia arvensis*) Blue-buttons. From England.

LADY'S LOCKETS—(*Adlumia
fungosa*) Fumitory. From England.

LADY'S NEEDLEWORK—
(*Cardamine pratensis*) Lady's
smock. From England.

LADY'S NEEDLEWORK—
(*Centranthus ruber*) Red valerian.
From England.

LADY'S NEEDLEWORK—(*Conium
maculatum*) Hemlock, California
fern. From England.

LADY'S PINCUSHION—(*Viburnum
opulus*) Guelder rose. From
England.

LADY'S SIGNET—(*Bryonia dioica*)
Red bryony.

LADY'S SIGNET—(*Polygonatum
multiflorum*) Solomon's-seal.

LADY'S SPURS—(*Consolida
ambigua*) Larkspur. In Spanish,
Espuelas de Dama.

LADY'S THIMBLE—(*Campanula
rotundifolia*) Bluebell. From
England.

LADY'S THIMBLE—(*Digitalis
purpurea*) Foxglove. From
England.

MADONNA'S PINS—(*Erodium
gruinum*) Heron's-bill. Pin-like,
thin, pointed seed pods form
following long-blooming violet
blossoms.

MADONNA'S PINS—(*Geranium
maculatum*) Wild geranium.

MADONNA'S PINS—(*Geranium
variety*) Scented geranium.
From Sicily.

MARY'S BELL—(*Campanula
medium*) Canterbury bells.

MARY'S CANDLE or MARY'S
TAPER—(*Verbascum thapsus*)
Great mullein. Candelabra-like
foliage and long, slender, candle-
like heads of yellow blossoms. In
France and Belgium known as *Le
Cierge de Notre Dame*, in Germany
as *Marien Kerzen* or *Unser Frauen
Heil*, in Gaelic as *Cuineal Mhuire.*
The top of the stalk in the female
plant "resembleth a torch decked
with infinite white floures."

MARY'S COIN—(*Chrysanthemum
balsamita*) Costmary, mint geranium. From Germany.

MARY'S DRINK—(*Arnica montana*)
Mountain tobacco. From
Germany. Possibly associated with
Mary because of the beneficial
healing effects of this plant.

MARY'S GOLD—(*Calendula officinalis*) Pot marigold.

MARY'S GOLD—(*Caltha palustris*) Marsh marigold. From England.

MARY'S LADDER—(*Centaurium erythraea*) Centaury. In Gaelic, *Dreimire Mhuire*.

MOTHER OF GOD'S TEA—(*Marrubium vulgare*) White horehound.

OUR LADY'S BASIN—(*Dipsacus fullonum*) Wild teasel. Leaves growing around the stem unite at the base to form a basin for dew or rain.

OUR LADY'S BEDS—(*Galium verum*) Yellow bedstraw. From England.

OUR LADY'S BELLS—(*Adenophera confusa*) Ladybells. Nodding bluebell blossoms. Angelus bells were once known as Our Lady's Bells.

OUR LADY'S BELLS—(*Campanula medium*) Canterbury bells. More than fifty types of bells dedicated to her, whether as shoes, slippers, gloves or thimbles, remind of her.

OUR LADY'S BELLS—(*Galanthus nivalis*) Common snowdrop. From England.

OUR LADY'S CANDLES—(*Castanea sativa*) European chestnut flowers. Tall yellowish flowers remind of candles; when blowing they seem to be decorating a shrine.

OUR LADY'S CANDLES—(*Silene alba*) White campion. From England.

OUR LADY'S CANDLESTICK—(*Primula elatior*) Primrose. Named from the erect stems and upwards facing flowers.

OUR LADY'S CHEESES—(*Malva sylvestris*) High mallow, cheeses.

OUR LADY'S CHEESES—(*Althaea officinalis*) Marsh mallow.

OUR LADY'S CUSHION—(*Arabis caucasica*) Wall rock cress. From England.

OUR LADY'S CUSHION—(*Armeria maritima*) Thrift. From England.

OUR LADY'S CUSHION—(*Chrysosplenium oppositifolium*) Golden saxifrage. From England.

OUR LADY'S FLAVORING—(*Mentha pulegium*) Pennyroyal.

OUR LADY'S FLAX—(*Chrysanthemum balsamita*) Costmary, mint geranium. From Germany.

OUR LADY'S GARLEEK—(*Allium schoenoprasum*) Chives.

OUR LADY'S KEYS—(*Primula veris*) Cowslip. From England.

OUR LADY'S LACE—(*Galium odoratum*) Sweet woodruff. From England.

OUR LADY'S LOOKING GLASS—(*Legousia speculum-Veneris*) Venus's-looking-glass. Associated first with Venus in pagan mythology then with Our Lady.

OUR LADY'S NEEDLE—(*Artemisia pontica*) Roman wormwood.

OUR LADY'S NEEDLEWORK—(*Saxifraga umbrosa*) Rockfoil, London-pride. From England.

OUR LADY'S PAINTBRUSH— (*Hieracium aurantiacum*) Orange hawkweed. Named from deep orange-red of flowers.

OUR LADY'S PINCUSHION— (*Armeria maritima*) Sea pink or thrift. Tufted cushion-like foliage and tall, pin-like blooms.

OUR LADY'S PINCUSHION— (*Scabiosa atropurpurea*) Sweet scabious, pincushions. Named for the small flower heads.

OUR LADY'S RIBBONS—(*Phalaris arundinacea*) Reed canary grass. Elegant strips look like ribbons.

OUR LADY'S SEAL— (*Cephalanthera*) Orchid variety. In Spanish, *Sello de Nostra Senora*.

OUR LADY'S SEAL—(*Smilacena racemosa*) False spikenard. Named from signet-like scar left on top of root stock by each year's shoots after they wither in the winter.

OUR LADY'S STICK—(*Lonicera xylosteum*) European fly honeysuckle. From Germany.

OUR LADY'S THIMBLE— (*Campanula rotundifolia*) Bluebell. Bell-shaped blooms on slender stems.

SAINT JOSEPH'S STAFF—(*Alcea rosea*) Hollyhock.

SAINT JOSEPH'S STAFF— (*Butomus umbellatus*) Flowering rush. In Spanish, *Vara de San Jose*.

SAINT JOSEPH'S STAFF— (*Narcissus jonquilla*) Jonquil. In Spanish, *Vara de Joseph*.

SAINT MARY'S SEAL—(*Convallaria species*) Lily of the valley. In Spanish, *Sello de Santa Maria*.

❧ In Mary's Garden ❧

HOLY HERB—(*Salvia sclarea*) Clary. In Spanish, *Hierba Santa*.

LADY OF THE MEADOW— (*Filipendula ulmaria*) Meadowsweet, Queen of the Meadow. From England.

LADY PALM—(*Rhapis excelsa*) Slender lady palm. From tropical America.

LADY'S CARROT—(*Ononis species*) Rest-harrow. In Spanish, *Carreton de Damas*.

LADY'S POSIES—(*Trifolium pratense*) Red clover. From England.

LADY'S SORREL—(*Oxalis acetosella*) European wood sorrel. From England.

MADONNA'S HERB—(*Glecoma hederacea*) Ground ivy. From England.

MARY'S CACTUS—(*Opuntia rosarica*) Prickly pear. From tropical America.

MARY'S CLOVER—(*Taenida integerrima*) Yellow pimpernel. In Gaelic, *Seamar Mhuire*.

MARY'S CRESS—(*Veronica beccabunga*) European brooklime. In Gaelic, *Biolar Mhuire*.

MARY'S FLOWER—(*Bellis perennis*) English daisy. White to rose blossoms in early spring.

MARY'S FLOWER—(*Petrea arborea*) Queen's-wreath. From tropical America.

MARY'S GARLIC—(*Allium ursinum*) Ramsons. In Gaelic, *Gairleog Mhuire*.

MARY'S NETTLE—(*Nepeta cataria*) Catnip, catmint.

MARY'S ROOT—(*Pastinaca sativa*) Parsnip. From Germany.

MARY'S SAXIFRAGE—(*Saxifraga granulata*) Meadow saxifrage. In Gaelic, *Mionan Mhuire*.

MOTHER OF GOD LILY—(*Convallaria majalis*) Lily of the valley. From Spain.

OUR LADY OF THE LAKE—(*Nymphaea alba*) European white water lily. From England.

OUR LADY'S BALSAM or **MARY'S LEAF**—(*Chrysanthemum balsam*) Costmary. Also called Bible Leaf because the leaves were sometimes used as Bible bookmarks. Combines fragrance of mint, lemon and balsam.

OUR LADY'S FENNEL—(*Foeniculum vulgare dulce*) Sweet fennel. From Germany.

OUR LADY'S FERN—(*Athyrium filix-femina*) Ladyfern. Long bright green leaves.

OUR LADY'S FLOWER—(*Anagallis grandiflora*) Blue pimpernel. The female of the species bears blue flowers.

OUR LADY'S MINT—(*Chrysanthemum balsamita*) Mint geranium. From Germany.

OUR LADY'S MINT—(*Mentha spicata*) Spearmint. In French, *Menthe de Notre Dame*. In Italian, *Herba Santa Maria*. In England, all mints were dedicated to the "Ladye Marye." In Italy, it is said to flower at the birthday of Mary in September and again on Christmas.

OUR LADY'S PLANT—(*Tanacetum vulgare*) Common tansy. In Spain, *Herba de Nosa Senora*.

OUR LADY'S SPRIG—(*Pimpinella anisum*) Anise.

ROSARY PLANT—(*Canna indica*) Indian-shot. In Spanish, *Yerbo de Rosaris*.

SAINT MARY'S CLOVER—(*Melilotus alba*) White sweet clover. In Spanish, *Trebol de Santa Maria*.

SAINT MARY'S TREE—(*Rosmarinus officinalis*) Rosemary. From England.

THE VIRGIN'S PALM—(*Dioon edule*) Chestnut dioon. From tropical America.

VIRGIN'S BOWER—(*Clematis virginiana*) Clematis, Virgin's-bower. From England.

WHERE GOD HAS WALKED—(*Glecoma hederacea*) Ground ivy. From England.

❧ Mary's Roses ❧

The rose for centuries has been associated with Mary, in religious painting and writing and also in the liturgical sense as in the petition, "Mystical Rose, pray for us." Those flowers referred to as "Mary's Rose" or used in place of the rose are included in this section. The roses for which there are legends are also included in Part Two.

CARNATION—(*Dianthus caryophyllus*) Divine flower. Used in many regions in place of the rose as an emblem of our Lady.

CHRISTMAS ROSE—(*Helleborus niger*) Christmas rose. From England.

MADONNA ROSE—(*Rosa odorata erubescens*) Tea rose hybrid. Often called monthly rose or daily rose because of its recurrent flowering.

MARY'S ROSE—(*Adonis aestivalis*) Pheasant's eye. One of several red flowers associated with Mary, the Mystical Rose of Heaven. From Germany.

MARY'S ROSE—(*Bellis perennis*) English daisy.

MARY'S ROSE—(*Lychnis coronaria*) Rose campion.

MARY'S ROSE— (*Paeonia lactiflora*) Common garden peony. From Germany.

MARY'S ROSE—(*Rosa canina*) Dog rose.

MARY'S ROSE—(*Silene, Dianthus barbatus*) Catchfly, sweet william.

MYSTIC ROSE—(*Rosa species*) Rose. From England.

OUR LADY'S ROSE—(*Rosa spinosissima*) Scotch rose. A variety of rose associated with Mary, the Mystical Rose of Heaven.

QUEEN MARY'S ROSE—(*Rosa eglanteria*) Sweetbrier. In Gaelic, *Ros na Bainriona Mhuire.*

ROSE OF HEAVEN—(*Lychnis coelirosa*) Rose-of-heaven. In Spanish, *Rosa del Cielo.*

ROSE OF JERICHO—(*Anastatica hierochuntica*) Our Lady's Rose.

ROSE OF JERICHO—(*Helianthus annuus*) Sunflower mirasol. From Italy.

ROSE DE NOEL—(*Eranthis hyemalis*) Winter aconite. From the French. Its golden blossoms lift to the Christmas sun.

ROSE OF SHARON—(*Hibiscus syriacus*) Shrub althea. A Chinese plant now known as Rose of Sharon, a title applied to our Lady from the Song of Solomon.

ROSE OF SHARON—(*Hypericum calycinum*) Creeping Saint-John's-wort

ROSE OF SHARON—(*Tulipa sharonensis*) Tulip. Thought to be the "Rose of Sharon" mentioned in the Song of Solomon.

SAINT MARY'S WILD ROSE— (*Paeonia broteri*) Peony. In Spanish, *Rosa de Santa Maria y del Monte.*

THE VIRGIN'S ROSE—(*Rosa centifolia*) Cabbage rose.

Bibliography

Adams, William Howard, *Nature Perfected*: Gardens through History, Abbeville Press, New York, 1991.

Addison, Josephine, *The Illustrated Plant Lore*, Sidgwick & Jackson, London, 1985.

Anderson, Frank J., *An Illustrated Treasury of Cultivated Flowers*, Abbeville Press, New York, 1979.

Asayama, Father Luke M., "*Report on the Virgin Mary in Intellectual and Spiritual Formation*," unpublished paper, 1998.

Ball, Ann, *Catholic Traditions in the Garden*, Our Sunday Visitor Publishing Division, Huntington, Ind., 1998.

___, "Mary Gardens," *Our Sunday Visitor*, vol. 81, no. 4, May 24, 1992.

Bayard, Tania, *Sweet Herbs and Sundry Flowers: Medieval Gardens and the Gardens of The Cloisters*, New York, Metropolitan Museum of Art, David R. Godine, Boston, 1985.

Berrall, Julia S., *The Garden, An Illustrated History*, Viking Press, New York, 1966.

Bourne, Eleanor, *Heritage of Flowers*, G.P. Putnam's Sons, New York, 1980.

Buby, Bertrand, S.M., *Mary, the Faithful Disciple*, Paulist Press, New York, 1985.

___, *Mary of Galilee: Mary in the New Testament*, Alba House, New York, 1994.

___, *Mary of Galilee: The Marian Heritage of the Early Church*, Alba House, New York, 1997.

Bunyard, Edward A., *Old Garden Roses*, Earl M. Coleman, New York, 1978.

Cecil, The Hon. Mrs. Evelyn, *A History of Gardening in England*, E.P. Dutton and Co., New York, 1910.

Clarke, Egerton, *Our Lady of the Flowers*, Burns Oates and Washburne, Ltd., London, 1937.

Clarkson, Rosetta E., *Green Enchantment: The Magic Spell of Gardens*, Macmillan Company, New York, 1940.

___, *Magic Gardens*, originally published 1939, Collier Books, New York, 1992.

Cloutham, Jeremy, "Gardens for Mary," *Columbia*, March, 1953.

Coats, Alice M., *Flowers and their Histories*, McGraw-Hill, New York, 1968.

Codrington, John, *The Cloister Garden of Lincoln Cathedral*, Lincoln, England.

Cowen, Painton, *Rose Windows*, Chronicle Books, San Francisco, 1979.

Crisp, Frank, *Medieval Gardens*, Hacker Art Books, New York, 1966.

Cruttwell, Maud, *Luca & Andrea della Robbia and Their Successors*, J. M. Dent & Co., London, 1902.

Cunneen, Sally, *In Search of Mary: The Woman and the Symbol*, Ballantine Books, New York, 1996.

Damrosch, Barbara, *Theme Gardens*, Workman Publishing, New York, 1982.

Dowling, Alfred E.P. Raymund, *The Flora of the Sacred Nativity*, Kegan Paul, Trench, Trubner & Co., Ltd., London, 1900.

Dutton, Ralph, *The English Garden*, B.T. Batsford Ltd., London, 1938.

Eva, Sister Mary, OSF, *The Garden Enclosed*, Benziger Brothers, New York, 1936.

Ewart, Neil, *The Lore of Flowers*, Blandford Press Poole, Dorset, England, 1982.

Friend, Hilderic, FLS, *Flowers and Flower Lore*, Vol. I, George Allen & Co., London, 1883.

Galvin, James J., C.SS.R., "My Garden Prays," *Perpetual Help*, February, 1952.

___, "Lillie Tower," *Perpetual Help*, August, 1946.

Gay, John, *Poetry and Prose*, Vol. 1, ed. by Vinton A. Dearing, Oxford University Press, London, 1974.

Gemminger, Louis, *Flowers of Mary: Addresses in Honor of the Blessed Virgin Mary*, translated by a Benedictine Sister, John Murphy & Co., Baltimore, 1894.

Gerard, John, Herbal: *The History of Plants*, ed. by Marcus Woodward, originally published 1927; Studio Editions Ltd, London, 1994.

Gibbs, Rebecca Whitehead, *Gardens Through the Ages*, c. by author, 1937.

Gilmer, Maureen, *Rooted in the Spirit*, Taylor Publishing Co., Dallas, 1997.

Goody, Jack, *The Culture of Flowers*, Cambridge University Press, Mass., 1993.

Gordon, Lesley, *Green Magic: Flowers Plants and Herbs in Lore and Legend*, Viking Press, New York, 1977.

Greenoak, Francesca, *God's Acre*, E.P. Dutton, New York, 1985.

Grimm, Jacob, *Teutonic Mythology*, translated from the fourth edition by James S. Stallybrass, Dover Publications, Inc., New York, 1966.

Haig, Elizabeth, *Floral Symbolism of the Great Masters*, Kegan Paul, Trench, Trubner and Co. Ltd., London, 1913.

Harvey, John, *Mediaeval Gardens*, Timber Press, Oregon, 1981.

Henshaw, Julia P., ed., *The Detroit Institute of Arts: A Visitor's Guide*, Wayne State University Press, Detroit, Mich., 1995.

Herolt, Johannes, *Miracles of the Blessed Virgin Mary*, translated from the Latin by C. C. Swinton Bland, George Routledge & Sons, Ltd., London, 1928.

Hobhouse, Penelope, *Gardening Through the Ages*, Simon and Schuster, New York, 1992.

Hollingsworth, Buckner, *Flower Chronicles*, Rutgers University Press, New Brunswick, New Jersey, 1958.

Hollister, C. Warren, *Medieval Europe: A Short History*, John Wiley & Sons, Santa Barbara, Calif., 1978.

Holmes, George, ed., *The Oxford Illustrated History of Medieval Europe*, Oxford University Press, Oxford, 1988.

Hurll, Estelle M., *The Madonna in Art*, L.C. Page & Co., Boston, 1897.

Ickis, Marguerite, *The Book of Religious Holidays and Celebrations*, Dodd, Mead & Co., New York, 1966.

Jablonski, Ramona, *The Medieval Garden Design Book*, Stemmer House, Owings Mills, Md., 1982.

Jamison, Mrs. (Anna), *Legends of the Madonna as Represented in the Fine Arts*, London: Longmans, Green, and Co., New York, 1890. Republished by Omnigraphics, Detroit, Mich.,1990.

Jenner, Mrs. Henry, *Our Lady in Art*, A.C. McClung & Co., Chicago, 1910.

Jewett, Sophie (Francesca, Sister Mary, Obl. SF.), *Our Ladye's Garlands*, Phillip Allen, England, 1931.

Jones, Julia and Barbara Deer, *The Country Diary of Garden Lore*, Simon and Schuster, New York 1989.

Kightly, Charles, *The Customs and Ceremonies of Britain*, Thames and Hudson, London, 1986.

Koepke, Ann, *Herbs and Flowers in the Bible*, Forward Movement Publications, Cincinnati, 1990.

Krymow, Vincenzina, "Gardeners Remember Mary with Flowers," *Catholic Telegraph*, vol. 163, no. 18, May 6, 1994.

_____, "Mary's Gardens Grow on the Internet," *Catholic Telegraph*, vol. 165, no. 19, May 10, 1996.

Kuppers, Leonhard, *Mary*, translated from German by Hans Hermann Rosenwald, Aurel Bongers, Recklinhausen, West Germany, 1965.

Landsberg, Sylvia, *The Medieval Garden*, Thames and Hudson, New York, 1996.

Lane, Peggy, "The Miracle on Albion Avenue," *Cincinnati Enquirer*, 1982.

Lehner, Ernst and Johanna, *Folklore and Symbolism of Flowers, Plants and Trees*, Tudor Publishing Co., New York, 1960.

Levi D'Ancona, Mirella, *The Garden of the Renaissance: Botanical Symbolism in Italian Painting*, Arte e Archeologia Studi e Documenti 10, Firenze, Italy, 1977.

MacNamara, Sean, C.F.C., " 'Mhuire' and 'Mary' Plants Growing Wild in Ireland," Knock Mary Garden, Ireland, 1987.

Martin, Laura C., *Garden Flower Folklore*, Globe Pequot Press, Old Saybrook, Conn., 1987.

Mary's Gardens Catalog, *Mary's Gardens*, Philadelphia, 1955.

Marzell, Heinrich, *Die Pflanzen im Deutchen Volksleben*, Eugen Diederichs, Jena, Germany, 1925.

Masson, Georgina, *Italian Gardens*, Antique Collectors' Club Ltd., Woodbridge, Suffolk, England, 1987.

Maugham, Mabel (Beldy), *Our Lady's Book of Flowers*, Assisi Press, Dublin, 1958.

McLaughlin, Jane A., "The Angelus Bell Tower and Mary Garden in Woods Hole," *Spritsail*, Vol. 6, No. 2, Summer 1992.

McLean, Teresa, *Medieval English Gardens*, The Viking Press, New York, 1980.

Mitchell, Vic, *Plants of the Bible*, Lion Publishing, England, 1978.

Moldenke, Harold N., "Flowers of the Madonna," *Horticulture*, December, 1953.

Newdick, Jane, *Period Flowers*, Crown Publishers Inc., New York, 1991.

Nichols, Rose Standish, *Italian Pleasure Gardens*, Dodd, Mead & Co., New York, 1928.

O'Brien, Rev. William D., *Life of the Blessed Virgin in Pictures*, Extension Press, Chicago, 1919.

Paterson, John & Katherine, *Consider the Lilies: Plants of the Bible*, Thomas Y. Crowell, New York, 1986.

Paterson, Wilma, *A Fountain of Gardens: Plants and Herbs of the Bible*, Mainstream Publishing Co. Ltd., Edinburgh, Scotland, 1990.

Pelikan, Jaroslav, *Mary Through the Centuries: Her Place in the History of Culture*, Yale University Press, New Haven, N.J., 1996.

Perry, Frances, *Flowers of the World*, Hamlyn Publishing Group Limited, London, 1972.

Pope John Paul II, "Mulieris Dignitatem," *"On the Dignity and Vocation of Women,"* Apostolic Letter, Vatican translation, St. Paul Books and Media, Boston, 1988.

Reimer, Susan, *"Seeds of Devotion,"* Baltimore Sun, June 4, 1995.

Roberson, Bonnie, "Mary Gardens," *Queen*, March, 1977.

Roberson, Bonnie and John Stokes, Jr., "Mary Gardens: The Herbs and Flowers of the Virgin Mary," *The Herbarist*, 1983."

Rohde, Eleanour Sinclair, *The Story of the Garden*, Hale, Cushman & Flint, Inc., Boston, 1932

Ruether, Rosemary Radford, "Mary in U.S. Catholic Culture," *National Catholic Reporter*, Feb. 10, 1995.

Seward, Barbara, *The Symbolic Rose*, Columbia University Press, New York, 1960.

Shewell-Cooper, W.E., *Plants, Flowers and Herbs of the Bible*, Keats Publishing Co., New Canaan, Conn., 1988.

Simmons, Adelma G., *Herb Gardens of Delight*, Hawthorn Books, Inc., New York, 1974.

Smith, Judith, *The Mary Calendar*, St. Dominic's Press, Ditchling, 1930.

Staff of the L.H. Bailey Hortorium, Cornell University, *Hortus Third: A Concise Dictionary of Plants Cultivated in the United States and Canada*, Macmillan Publishing Company, Inc., New York, 1976.

Stanley, Thomas A., S.M., "*Mary's Garden*," St. Catherine of Siena Church, Portage, Mich., 1993.

Stokes, John S., Jr., "*The Blessing of Mary Gardens as Holy Places*," Mary Gardens Home Page, http://www.mgardens.org, 1996.

___, "A Garden Full of Aves," reprinted from *The Marianist*, University of Dayton.

___, "*Flower Theology*," Mary Gardens Home Page, 1995.

___, "Mary Garden Jubilee," *Queen*, May-June 1982.

___, "Mary Garden Research: A Progress Report," *Queen*, Feb. 1955.

___, "Paradise of Our Lady," *Queen*, May-June 1988.

Stokes, John S. Jr., and Winifred J. Emerson, *Mariana 1*, unpublished manuscript.

Stokstad, Marilyn, and Jerry Stannard, *Gardens of the Middle Ages, Catalogue for the Exhibition*, Spencer Museum of Art, The University of Kansas, Lawrence, Kan. 1983.

Sullivan, Robert, "The Mystery of Mary," *Life*, December, 1996.

Tergit, Gabriele, *Flowers Through the Ages*, translated from the German by Elizabeth and Alexander Henderson, Oswald Wolff Ltd., London, 1961.

Thacker, Christopher, *The History of Gardens*, University of California Press, Berkeley, Calif., 1979.

Toledo Museum of Art, *Toledo Treasures*, Hudson Hills Press, New York, 1995.

Valdes, Marquesa de Casa, *Spanish Gardens*, Antique Collectors' Club, Ltd., Woodbridge, Suffolk, England, 1987.

Vercelloni, Virgilio, *European Gardens: A Historical Atlas*, Rizzoli, New York, 1990.

Verite, Marcelle, *Gardens Through the Ages*, Odhams Books, Ltd., London, 1964.

Voragine, Jacobus de, *The Golden Legend*, translated and adapted from the Latin by Granger Ryan and Helmut Ripperger, Arno Press, New York, 1969.

Warner, Marina, *Alone of All Her Sex: The Myth and the Cult of the Virgin Mary*, Alfred A. Knopf, New York, 1976.

Weiser, Francis X., *The Christmas Book*, Harcourt, Brace and Co., New York, 1952.

___, *Handbook of Christian Feasts and Customs*, Harcourt, Brace and Co., New York, 1952.

___, *The Holy Day Book*, Harcourt, Brace and Co., New York, 1956.

Wilkins, Eithne, *The Rose Garden Game: A Tradition of Beads and Flowers*, Herder and Herder, New York, 1969.

Wright, Richardson, *The Story of Gardening*, Dodd, Mead and Co., New York, 1934.

Wyman, Donald, *Wyman's Gardening Encyclopedia*, MacMillan Publishing Company, Inc., New York, 1977.

Index